Rhodes

A Notebook

Lives and Landscapes on the Island of Roses

By Richard Clark

By The Same Author:

The Greek Islands – A Notebook

ISBN: 9781466285316   ASIN: B005O044PS

Crete – A Notebook

ISBN: 9781475188943   ASIN: B008N9ES1M

First published in America and Great Britain 2013
Copyright © 2013 by Richard Clark
Book design and layout © 2013 by Cheryl Perez
Cover design © by David Richardson 2013

All rights reserved. No part of this publication can be reproduced or transmitted in any form or by any means, electronic or mechanical, without permission in writing from Richard Clark.

ISBN – 13:9781483971285
ISBN – 10:1483971287

www.richardclarkbooks.co.uk

Praise for **The Greek Islands – A Notebook**

'This is a beautifully written book, not just a travel companion but a journey in itself through Greek History, its culture and the countryside. Reading this book is an education in itself and I found myself so much the richer for having read it.'

E.J. Russell, *bestselling author of Return to the Aegean*

'What I liked most about the book was that it was personal and with that came an honesty, no wrappings, no embellishments other than descriptions of Greece itself. I would recommend this book both to people who have never been to Greece as well as to seasoned travellers. It was a joy.'

Sarah Alexi, *bestselling author of The Illegal Gardener; Black Butterflies; The Explosive Nature of Friendship*

'My library contains almost all of the noteworthy books about Greece and her islands and this will be a welcomed addition. I will place it next to my collection of books by the late and great Patrick Leigh Fermor, because I think Richard Clark's writing is as close to Fermor as we will ever come again.'

Aurelia Smeltz, *author of Labyrinthine Ways, A Lone Red Apple*

Praise for *Crete – A Notebook*

'I was really surprised and delighted by the book. I read every word. The author is a fine writer and describes the island vividly. It's not a guidebook although there's a lot of information here that should be in any good guidebook. He travels around the island in clockwise direction, writing short essays as he goes, which are a mix of personal memoir, history, and an evocation of place. The last one he does very well, as it brought back memories to me of my own travels around the island. He really does capture places well.'

Mike Gerrard, *author of AA Spiral Guide to Crete*

'I love the way Clark writes, it is personal, it is human and deceptively simple. A book crafted so carefully you almost believe that it's a notebook, were it not for the flow.'

Sarah Alexi, *bestselling author of The Illegal Gardener; Black Butterflies; The Explosive Nature of Friendship*

'Unsurprisingly, travel literature constitutes the vast majority of my reading these days, and I devour as much online and off as I can. In examining other writers' style and content, I have become accustomed to dipping in and out of work. The extent to which I have been unable to put Richard Clark's book down is a tribute to its compulsive readability.'

Travel journalist **Emma French,**
www.phileasfrench.com

For My Mother

Acknowledgements

Rhodes – A Notebook is my third book about the Greek Islands. It focuses on an island of which I have fond memories and still visit whenever I can. It is intended to be a memoir, so if I have in some instances misremembered any detail I am sorry and apologize in advance. My previous two books have taken on a life of their own, and I am amazed and humbled by their success, so I say a heartfelt thank you to anyone who has bought them. I also must thank fellow authors Mark Hudson, Sara Alexi, E.J. Russell and Aurelia Smeltz for their kind words and encouragement. Some of the articles about Rhodes and island life were previously published in my first book and, for those of you who have read that, I ask for your forbearance. Rhodes is an island, the very essence of which is bound up in myth and legend and these are very much open to interpretation. My version of any mythological events is by no means definitive and I hope any discrepancies in detail will not compromise the integrity of the book. Some names of people in the book have also been changed.

I would like to thank again Barney Harsent for his patience and editing skills, similarly Cheryl Perez who brings my books to life with her design and formatting expertise for both the print and eBook versions, and David Richardson for another arresting cover design and, as always, my family, Denise, Rebecca and James.

Rhodes – A Notebook

Lives and Landscapes on the Island of Roses

Those of you who are familiar with my previous two books, *The Greek Islands – A Notebook* and *Crete – A Notebook*, may notice a pattern emerging. I suspect this has turned into a series, and nobody is more surprised than me. When I first set out to write about my experiences in Greece I was not sure I had enough material to complete just one book; and even if I had that so many people would want to read about them.

I discovered, tucked away in the corners of my mind, more recollections than I realized, and the process of writing brought them to the fore. As before, this book contains snapshots of experiences I have had, places I have visited and things I have learned on my trips to Rhodes, a place I first visited in the 1980s. Like the other books this is not supposed to be a guide, but more a series of personal impressions of an island that I have been fortunate enough to visit on numerous occasions. That being said, I hope I will have done enough through my writing to encourage readers to take a journey and discover more about the people, places and culture which make up this beautiful 'island of roses'.

Rhodes – The Island of the Knights

With a fair wind, the island of Rhodes is but half a day's voyage by ferry from Piraeus. Athens' seaport lies some 250 miles to the north west of this jewelled island that nestles little more than a stone's throw away from Asia and the Turkish coast. At 11 miles from the natural homeland of the old Ottoman Empire, Rhodes, the largest of the Dodecanese archipelago, has for millennia been subject to the push and pull of the tides of political fortune in this south-eastern corner of the Aegean Sea. Although the fourth largest of the Greek Islands, it is small enough to be easily explored, its landscape benign, yet abundant enough in variety to hold the attention for a lifetime.

If that vista exudes a timeless quality, the intervention of buildings and archaeological finds betrays the island's turbulent past. But in the context of modern Greece, Rhodes and the other islands of the Dodecanese were the final piece in the jigsaw, the last part of this intricate picture to be put into place. It was not until after the Second World War, in 1947, that the defeated Italian rulers were officially made to hand over the islands. Rhodes and its satellites were finally reunited with the newly reformed, independent Greek state which had been pulling itself together for the previous 135 years.

Lawrence Durrell, in *Reflections on a Marine Venus*, his classic memoir about post-war Rhodes, writes of the difficulties of expressing the essence of the Island: 'In Rhodes the days drop as softly as fruit from the trees. Some belong to the dazzling ages of Cleobulus and the tyrants, some to the gloomy Tiberius, some to the Crusaders. They follow each other in scales and modes too quickly to be captured in the nets of form.'

The difficulty lies in trying to find an identity that fits. The island has changed its clothes so many times throughout history that it is hard to identify the fashion which best reflects its character. Inhabited since the Neolithic period, the Minoans came here in the 16th Century BC but did not leave their mark in the same way that they had further to the south west in Crete. The Telchines are held in some legends to have been the first inhabitants. The offspring of Gaia and Pontus, they hailed from Crete. These children of the gods had magical powers and were skilled metalworkers who created Poseidon's trident, and a sickle for Cronos. In certain accounts their children were Ialyssos, Lindos and Kamiros. This theory is at odds with another that claims these boys, who gave their name to the triumvirate of early Rhodian cities, were the sons of Danaus. To make it more confusing, the poet Pindar wrote down the myth that is perhaps most widely accepted. He claims that the aforementioned children were the fruit of the union between Aphrodite and Helios, and it was their daughter, Rhodes, who lent her name to the island.

It is almost impossible to find any two accounts that concur. Frustrated by the failure of my research, I am forced to recall my friend Theo's thoughts on the matter. Usually adroit, he would frequently remind me with a certainty that only a few glasses of ouzo can engender, that the ancient Greeks were promiscuous in their interpretations of the myths, so it is reasonable that we too can pick and mix our legends.

Pindar was something of a revisionist himself, however. On the flimsiest of evidence, he cites Helios as the father of our eponymous heroes, who himself was worshipped across the island and was celebrated by the magnificent Colossus, one of the Seven Wonders of the Ancient World. Bearing this in mind, Pindar just edges it. That Rhodes' airport is named after the Olympic boxer Diagoras, in whose honour Pindar wrote the *Seventh Olympian Ode* which recalls the myth, further reinforces the case!

The subject of the poem epitomizes the glories of sporting achievement and the joy in sharing the success of others. In the 5th Century BC, Diagoras won the boxing event at the Olympic Games twice, but at the 83rd Olympiad in 448BC, two of his sons also became champions. In celebration, they hoisted their father aloft and carried him around the arena. This was held to be the most contented a man could be and, from the standing crowd, a spectator is believed to have shouted, 'You can die now Diagoras, as Mount Olympus you will not climb', with which the proud father did indeed drop dead, a happy man, we are led to believe. The occasions I have arrived at the airport named after the famed boxer have often been far from happy – bomb scares and delays of Herculean proportions, along with the resulting exhaustion, have influenced my decision to arrive on the island by boat.

My ship cast off from Piraeus in the early evening. By the time dusk fell, the breeze created by the ferry pushing south left a chill on the spring air. The lights of Athens rode the waves like a giant cruise liner disappearing over the horizon. The sky was ablaze with stars given full license to shine their brightest in the darkest of blue-black skies. Occasionally a cluster of lights from some small island would appear like a mystical galaxy adrift in a watery universe.

Pulling on a jumper and sitting in the lee of a lifeboat, the moment was laced with anticipation, the regular drumming of the engines beating out the only accompaniment to my thoughts. Eventually letting the cold get the better of me, I descended the steel steps to the saloon and claimed a spot where I could stretch out for the night. Some cheese pies, a sweet Greek coffee and Metaxa lulled me into a sound sleep on my bench seat, until a hint of sunlight through the overhead porthole shook me awake, calling me on deck to see the emerging dawn. Off our starboard bow the lights were going out as Rhodes town rose from its slumbers.

From several miles out it was already showing off its splendours, the crenellations of battlements and its minarets and domes silhouetted against the encroaching dawn. It is an enticing sight. But one that only welcomes those who come in peace, for the defenses of the town are formidable and the history of the island is one of siege. We coast along past the imposing city walls and the ancient windmills which grace the harbour of Mandraki before turning hard to starboard; winches grinding we come alongside in the commercial port just to the east of the old town.

It is an overwhelming, medieval aura that distinguishes Rhodes from its island cousins; it is not the sun-bleached, dusty antiquity of ancient Greece, but the gothic that takes precedence here. And for the old city of Rhodes, which is now a World Heritage Site, it is reluctantly Mussolini's black-shirted revisionists and their unhealthy preoccupation with the chivalric traditions of the Knights, that we must credit for much of the restoration of the town.

To access it now from the harbour is simple. A stroll through any of the vast gates that punctuate the walls delivers you into a different world. The Knights themselves took the island after a two-year siege in 1309, succeeding where the great Macedonian King Demetrius I had failed some 1600 years previously. Known as Poliorcetes (the siege maker), he turned his attentions to the strategically important centre of Rhodes in punishment for them not having supported him in his successful campaigns against the Egyptians and Cypriots. His flagship led a massive fleet of warships, carrying an invasion force of more than 40,000 troops, double what the Rhodians could muster to defend their birthright.

With an impressive armoury including a battering ram – at 180 feet long so huge it took more than 1000 soldiers to wield it – and a siege tower called Helepolis (conqueror of cities) weighing little under 200 tons and standing 125 feet tall, he led an assault on the town which proved futile. A year of huffing and puffing was enough, after which Poliorcetes turned, weighed anchor and set sail for Athens. The bravery of the islanders had left such a mark on the Macedonian that he deserted Helepolis as a token of respect for his worthy adversaries, making him an unlikely benefactor. The melted down scrap was used in the building of the great Colossus of Rhodes, dedicated to the god, Helios, who, Rhodians believed, had restored their fortunes in the war.

On the run from the Knights Templar following infighting between the chivalric orders, the Knights

Hospitaller dragged its wounded rump from Cyprus to Rhodes. Seeing its potential as a stronghold for the beleaguered order, they set siege to the island in 1307 and prevailed after two years of bitter conflict. Reinventing themselves as the Knights of Rhodes, they set about further reinforcing the island's already prodigious defenses, building a city in the image of their gothic ideal. And it is mostly the Knights' heritage which has been restored, firstly by the Italian invaders, and since by various more empathetic archaeological practitioners.

If the magnificent buildings were beautiful manifestations of the Hospitaller's arrogance, their longevity on the island surviving two great sieges is evidence that not all their swagger was misplaced. In 1444 the Sultan of Egypt tried his luck but was comprehensively repulsed. Thirty-six years later the Ottoman leader Sultan Mehmet II, or 'The Conquerer', failed to live up to his name and was driven back into the sea by the cavalry of the Knights commanded by Englishman John Kendal. Eventually in 1522 the Ottomans under Suleiman the Magnificent gained the territory they had cherished for centuries.

A force of some 100,000 finally prevailed over just 640 Knights and their ragbag band of supporters who had found themselves in the city and its surroundings at the time. By December the embattled Knights realized they were beaten and negotiated safe passage for the surviving 180 members of the order. On the 1st January 1523 they set sail for Crete before finally settling in Malta some six years later.

This began another era that left an indelible mark on the city. For almost 400 years, until 1912, Rhodes came under the panoply of the Ottoman Empire. Greeks were banished from within the great walls of the capital. This left behind only a Jewish settlement pitched under the defenses to the east, and the Turkish settlers who set about the Islamification of the town, turning all churches to mosques and erecting public buildings, of which the *hammam* or Turkish baths (now called Dhimotika Loutra) is a fine example. In this 17th-century Byzantine edifice in the south of the old town, with the sunlight streaming through star-shaped apertures in the towering cream dome of the baths, any visitor can still gain relief from the heat and dust of city life. A few euros can see you sweating it out by the olive wood fires, sitting on the same marble slabs as the Pashas did centuries before.

These days I prefer to take my refreshment in the Nea Agora (new market), a place I remember as being more open and light than it now appears. When I first visited here it was a dusty, airy space with random scruffy tables set out beneath the odd tree which emerged through dirt gaps in the squared paving slabs. The imperious domed entrance to this heptagonal building opposite the old harbour of Mandraki looks like the work of the Ottomans, which had spilled outside the walls of the old town. In fact it was the musing of Italian architect Florestan di Fausto, employed as an urban planner in Rhodes between 1922 and 1926 who was also responsible for the Governor's Palace further north along the coast road.

That the city developed outside the walls of the old town was a result of the expulsion of the indigenous citizens following Suleiman's ousting of the Knights. The Jewish settlers, however, were given leave to remain. They did so in peace for 422 years until the Gestapo rounded up most of the community and sent them to the death camps in 1944.

Much of the new town is a legacy of the Italians whose neo-Gothic and Venetian reveries make a pleasing, if on occasion incongruous, juxtaposition to the earlier medieval and Arabic styles. The archway supporting di Fausto's dome is resplendent in gold decoration and dominates the forefront of the harbour side. Looking back seawards, the defensive circular tower of the Knight's castle of Agios Nikolaos stands sentinel at the harbour mouth. In its shadow rise the two columns supporting a bronze stag and a doe on either side of the entrance to the old port. In times of conflict the harbour could be defended with underwater chains strung across its entrance to arrest the progress of invading ships. Inside the Nea Agora's walls the courtyard closes in on you. The tavernas and ouzeries of old have been supplemented by souvenir shops, flower beds and mature trees, all of which conspire to make it a pleasant place to sit on one of the many tables which spill out onto the centre of the courtyard. On my first visit I ate snails with a garlic aioli to dip, bread to tear and steely cold wine to drink, today we settle for a pizza and beer which was just as welcome.

The Lost Wonder

Before visiting Rhodes in the mid Eighties, the thing that resonated most about the island was the Colossus. It seems ironic that for many this island is famous for something that no longer exists, even as ruins, particularly as there is still much debate as to where it stood.

Built in the island capital of Rhodes Town, one of the Seven Wonders of the Ancient World, it took 12 years to construct and was finished in 280 BC. The statue was of the Greek sun god Helios and stood more than 100 feet tall. It was created by Chares, a local sculptor from nearby Lindos, commissioned to celebrate the islanders' successful defense of an invasion in 304 BC.

The giant statue was built largely from recast iron and bronze left behind by the besieging 40,000 strong army of Demetrius Poliorcetes when it was seen off by the forces of the ruling Ptolemy. The statue stood on a huge stone pedestal and was made of individually cast bronze plates held together by rivets and strengthened inside by iron rods. The legs would have been filled with rocks to ballast them.

The romantics among us would love to believe that the giant statue straddled the harbour entrance of Mandraki, between the walls where the deer of Rhodes now stand atop their columns, but this apocryphal story has been discredited as being impossible for any number of practical reasons. It is more likely that the statue was built somewhere near the port, although some archaeologists have suggested it may have stood as part of the Acropolis, situated on a hill overlooking the city.

Unfortunately the great statue, although a tremendous feat of engineering, only stood for 56 years. In 226 BC Rhodes suffered a massive earthquake that the Colossus, along with many of the island's buildings, was unable to withstand. Although the ruling Ptolemy III offered to fund its reconstruction, the people feared that they had in some way upset the god Helios and preferred to let the matter lie.

That the Colossus actually existed is not in doubt, there are numerous documented accounts of the remains of the statue which lay on the ground for a further 800 years. They disappeared at the time of Rhodes' occupation by Arab forces in 654 AD. There are stories that the remains were sold for scrap to a Jewish trader, but this has never been verified.

The architects who designed New York's Statue of Liberty were strongly influenced by the idea of what they believed the Colossus looked like. It is referenced by the

Emma Lazarus poem *The New Colossus*, which is inscribed on the plaque inside the newer statue's pedestal. In an attempt to bring more tourism to Rhodes the idea that the Colossus should be rebuilt has often been mooted and in 2008 it was agreed that this was to happen, although it is likely, considering the financial constraints that Greece is now under, that the realization of the project may be protracted.

Lawrence Durrell – Rhodes' Great Advocate

To the north of Mandraki harbour, in the part of the town inhabited by the fine administrative buildings erected by the Italians during the thirty-odd years they held sway here, is a little dwelling made famous as the house rented by the writer Lawrence Durrell. The celebrated author lived here for two years immediately following the end to hostilities with the Germans after the Second World War in 1945. The house nestles near the Grande Albergo Della Rosa hotel. Built in 1925, the hotel now houses the Rhodes Casino, but at the time was the headquarters of the British administration on the island.

If the Roses Hotel is famous for the signing of the treaty which saw the ceasefire between the newly created Jewish State of Israel and their Arab neighbours in 1949, this small gatekeeper's lodge in the secluded cemetery of the Mosque of Muraid Reis, being Durrell's erstwhile refuge, has its own, not insignificant, claim to fame. The road outside bustles with cars now. But it does not take too much of a leap of faith to imagine the small house with its courtyard garden as a secluded bolthole. Here Durrell could relax with his then partner, Eve Cohen, away from his job as the public administration officer for the island in the transitional period between its liberation in 1945 and *enosis* in 1947.

Durrell had spent the war years in Egypt, which was to be the inspiration for his most heralded work, *The Alexandria Quartet*, published between 1957 And 1960. But it is during his time here that the author claims to have been happier than at any other period of his life and on which he based his book, *Reflections on a Marine Venus – A Companion to the Landscape of Rhodes,* first published in 1953. A hidden hibiscus garden became Durrell's private space to entertain his friends and muse on the past and future of the 'Island of Roses'. He called his home Villa Cleobolus after the 6th Century BC governor of Lindos, one of the seven sages of great Greek thinkers heralded by Plato and Herodotus.

In his exquisite book *The Greek Islands*, published later in his life in 1978, Durrell writes of his time spent on Rhodes with less passion but no less affection than he does of his books about Corfu and Cyprus. The affable nature of the people and the benign beauty of the landscape affirms a sense of abundance. His contentment in his relationship with the island is more like that between good friends than passionate lovers, and it is easy to see why. Like no other Greek island, Rhodes has absorbed the vicissitudes of its past and proudly displays all its heritage, just as the Knights might have flown the Maltese cross from the highest ramparts of the Palace of the Grand Master. Perhaps the comfort of Durrell's wonderfully languid descriptions of the island have led to him being heralded here less than elsewhere in Greece. In Corfu he and his brother, Gerald, have a Garden in Kyrkyra named after them, here a plaque on the wall of Villa Cleobolus suffices.

'For two lucky years I was able, by virtue of my job with the occupying force, to swim at the Albergo Della Rosa beach and to inhabit a tiny studio buried in flowering hibiscus hard by – at the shrine of Murad Reis which still exists, though the old Mufti is dead and the cemetery terribly unkempt.'

Lawrence Durrell, *The Greek Islands*

The title of his book on Rhodes does not revere the great Colossus or indeed the Temple of Apollo that looks down on the old city from Monte Smith, the hillside acropolis incongruously named after a British admiral. His Marine Venus is coyly hidden away in the city's Archaeological Museum. With details of its provenance and history unclear, she has nevertheless been immortalised by Durrell as a symbol of the island, raised from the depths to find new hope after the dark days of war.

This is not the famed Bathing Aphrodite of Rhodes, who crouches nearby in the museum, drying her hair in the sunshine after emerging from the sea, but a real escapee from beneath the waves, or so local folklore would have it. Durrell's Venus was a smoothed Aphrodite Pudica, thought to be a cult statue from the temple to that same goddess which lies near what is now the commercial harbour. She was landed by fishermen in their nets, sea worn and battered; a catch that became imbued with lasting value. Buried for a second time, this time in some underground vault to hide her from the ravages of war, Durrell witnessed her re-emergence into the light again, liberated at last, and invested the statue with its timeless significance.

'So long as we are in this place we shall not be free from her; it is as if our thoughts must be forever stained by some of her own dark illumination – the preoccupation of a stone woman inherited from a past whose greatest hopes and ideals fell to ruins. Behind and through her the whole idea of Greece glows sadly, like some broken capital, like the shattered pieces of a graceful jar, like the torso of a statue to hope.'

Lawrence Durrell, *Reflections on a Marine Venus*

Durrell left the island in 1947, some years before he found international recognition as a writer, before moving to Cordoba in Argentina and on to Yugoslavia and Cyprus, on which he based his award-winning 1957 book *Bitter Lemons*. Forced out of Cyprus by the troubles between the Greek

Cypriots who wanted *enosis* with Greece and the British administration, a disillusioned Durrell settled in the South of France where he lived until his death in 1990. But even after having left the eastern Mediterranean he remembers Rhodes with great affection.

'There could be no pleasanter place to buy a cottage for the summer; I venture to think that of all the island climates I know, the Rhodian climate is the best in every sense... It was always with a pang that we took ships to leave Rhodes; the farewell siren echoed up there on Monte Smith and among the green glades of Callithea and Rodini with heartbreak in it.'

Lawrence Durrell, *The Greek Islands*

The City of the Knights

Approaching Rhodes Town from the sea on *Birba*, it was easy to imagine what confronted Sultan Suleiman the Magnificent's 100,000 troops aboard their 400 ships as they approached to lay siege to the city in 1522.

Shadows of the town's medieval fortifications loom defiantly over Mandraki Harbour, exuding romantic notions of chivalric knighthood. Today, aboard the little sloop silently cruising towards harbour it is one of the most beautiful island vistas in Greece but, to the Sultan's men, the picturesque splendour of the approach must have been outweighed by a terrible apprehension.

Much of the current town was built to meet the vision of the chivalric ideal by the crusading order of the Knights Hospitaller who renamed themselves the Knights of Rhodes after taking control of the city in 1309. We pass between the two pillars on top of which stand two deer, one male and one female, symbols of the island. This is the entrance to the harbour which some believe was, at one time, straddled by the Colossus.

Mooring up stern first we head ashore into the old city. In the heat of the day the alleyways and squares are deserted. We walk along the Street of the Knights where the warriors used to train and pray, from the New Hospital that now houses the archaeological museum to the magnificent Grandmaster's Palace. The medieval buildings are so well preserved that walking among them it is difficult not to imagine that you have been taken back in time.

Despite inflicting massive casualties on the invading Turks, the Knights finally faced the inevitable and agreed terms by which they would gain free passage from the city with all the wealth they could carry. In return the Greek population would be allowed to continue their Christian worship outside the city walls without retribution.

On departing the island the Knights found shelter on Crete and Sicily before moving to Malta and Gozo. The taking of Rhodes by the Turks was of tremendous strategic importance to the Ottoman Empire, giving them a staging post for their eventual rout of the Venetians in Crete a century and a half later in 1669.

Unlike in Crete, there was no great physical resistance to the Turks, which probably accounts for how well the old town is preserved. The Greek population was forced to move outside the city walls where they continued to worship in

Orthodox churches and made their living in the predominantly rural economy.

Within the city itself most of the churches were transformed into mosques; with domes and minarets being added to the existing structures. The Turkish baths, which still operate, were built, and existing medieval houses were augmented with the traditional enclosed wooden balconies much favoured in Ottoman architecture.

The Turks held Rhodes for nearly four centuries, but in 1912 their power was in decline. Whilst defending the Ottoman Empire in the First Balkan War against the league of the Christian states of Greece, Bulgaria, Serbia and Montenegro, Italy took its opportunity and seized the Dodecanese. Although a blow to any ambitions the islands had for *enosis*, or union with Greece, it did, however, keep them out of the traumatic exchange of population with Turkey following Greece's ill-fated campaign in Smyrna in 1922. In this year millions of Greeks and Muslims were uprooted from the country of their birth and relocated within the newly drawn borders of Greece and Turkey.

The signing of the Italian armistice following their defeat by the Allies in 1943 led to the occupation of Rhodes and the rest of the Dodecanese by the Germans. The next year they sent 1673 of the island's Jewish community to the death camps. Only some 150 survived. The islands were finally united with Greece after the signing of the post-war peace settlement in 1947.

As night falls, we sit drinking in the cockpit of *Birba*. The town again becomes the City of the Knights. The walls of their stronghold, now illuminated, dominate the skyline. Solid and impenetrable, it is difficult to see what other memory of this unique place at the far east of the Mediterranean could take precedence.

Faliraki – A Blemish on the Face of Paradise

For an island that has held out so resolutely against any number of invaders in the past, Rhodes has recently succumbed to an invasion that may have succeeded after being mistaken for friendly fire. Fortunately the worst of the collateral damage has been limited to one area. Here the perpetrators of this unwelcome invasion are hunkered down in concrete bunkers, being relieved regularly by a new contingent of hedonistic warriors every fortnight throughout the summer. I have briefly passed through Kavos on Corfu and Malia on Crete, so in the interests of fairness' felt I had to visit Rhodes' notorious party town of Faliraki. It is fair to say it deserves every bit of its dubious reputation. That Faliraki makes the other couple of hell holes look like visions of paradise in comparison is not to overstate the case. Even the perpetual sunshine of Rhodes fails to shed any favourable light on this facsimile of a inner city sink estate shamelessly shouting the odds on this otherwise beautiful coastline to the south of Rhodes' majestic old town.

Many people might consider my dismissal of these 'party towns' as unfair. I am aware that hundreds of thousands of tourists flock to these resorts every year and have a great time. There is no doubt that this stretch of the coast is beautiful, as are the beaches. The natural splendour of these places highlights the destructive influence of the incursion of generic US burger joints, fried chicken stores, faux pubs and cafes selling poor imitations of north European cuisine.

Following the death of an Irish tourist in 2003 the police have cracked down on the size of bar crawls organized by the holiday reps here and the number of venues they can visit. But tensions between doing the sensible thing and how much the local business people and the tour operators will tolerate in their endless chase for increased profit has meant that any change to the image of this resort has been negligible.

As I have said before of Malia, I cannot understand whether the development of this 'party town' is a disaster or an ingenious plot by the local authorities to confine the worst aspects of tourism to one area. A dangerous cocktail of the relentless pursuit of profit by Greek businessmen and unscrupulous tour operators and their staff and the unceasing hedonism of holidaymakers has created a living hell out of what was once a Garden of Eden.

Putting the genie back in the bottle is proving difficult. The authorities are fighting an ongoing battle to try and balance the need for locals to make a living and the integrity of the island as a tourist destination. The police are increasingly coming down hard on drunken, violent behavior in the resort, but as yet their strong-arm tactics have had little effect.

Elsewhere on the island the behaviour of tourists in the town, mainly British I am ashamed to say, is a topic of conversation returned to again and again by Rhodians. They are in turn both shocked at the behavior and grateful it is not in their back yard. Perhaps, occasionally, there may be just a hint of envy at the living to be made there!

To Symi by Sea

Birba edged her nose out of Mandraki Harbour and tensed, then pushed on ahead as the breeze and slight swell took hold of her. At the helm, my friend, Dean, rounded up to a reach and pulled in the sheet. The small yacht took up the strain and heeled slightly to leeward, then comfortably set course for Symi.

As the medieval walls of Rhodes Old Town slipped away astern, we settled into the cockpit for the 25-mile voyage. Conditions were perfect as we let out the trailing log. We were making about five knots over a sea reflecting a light so perfect no picture could ever do it justice.

Not having been out of harbour for a week, *Birba's* hull took up water where the sun-dried wood felt the sea again as her gunwhales dipped towards its surface. A pump every half-hour took care of the bilges, and any cold water sprayed on our faces and legs was a welcome respite from the midday sun relentlessly bouncing off the sea.

Panormitis Bay is as close to idyllic as it gets. Entering through its narrow mouth the natural harbour opened up, revealing a sheltered, enclosed cove. We dropped anchor 50 yards offshore and, through the crystal clear water, watched it settle into the seabed below. The sun had increased in strength, reflecting with eye-blinking intensity off the white-painted buildings ashore and the burnished metallic blue surface of the sea.

The stillness was palpable, only broken by the stop-start choruses of the cicadas ashore. The smell of the salt left on deck as the water evaporated blended with the aroma of thyme that laced the air. Pine trees grew up out of the parched rock which forms a backdrop to the village at the forefront of which, right on the seafront, lies the famous monastery.

This Greek Orthodox monastery dominates the village and is the second largest in the Dodecanese. At its heart is the tallest baroque bell tower in the world that overlooks the rest of the retreat, which was rebuilt in Venetian style in the 18th Century. These days Panormitis is a tourist boat destination either from Rhodes or Symi Town in the north of the island. It is well worth a visit by any means, but if you can make the journey by local bus or are lucky enough to approach on your own boat outside peak hours the tranquility is overwhelming.

We unlashed the inflatable tender from deck, launched it and rowed ashore. Mooring on the front near a taverna, we walked to the monastery. Through the gates we entered a haven of peace, the black and white paved courtyard dotted with potted trees and exotic plants.

Entering the church, the shaded cool provides some respite from the searing heat. The walls of the church are covered with iconography; the most spectacular being the glinting, silver-leafed representation of Archangel Michael of Panormitis to whom the monastery is dedicated. The angel is the island's patron saint and considered the protector of all sailors who go to sea across the Dodecanese.

Tradition has it that the archangel will grant favours if promised something in return. Failure to honour that due results in the angry angel performing obstructive miracles until it is fulfilled. Many a devout tour boat's captain will vouch for the efficacy of this by recounting how they have been unable to start their engines and leave the bay until requesting over the PA system that all their passengers keep any promises they might have made to Michael!

Outside the church but still within the walls of the monastery are two museums. One is an exhibition of religious artifacts and the other folk art. A memorial also stands to three monks and two teachers who were executed by German forces in 1944 for operating a radio to help British forces and Greek partisans in their resistance against the occupying power.

Back aboard, we find ourselves alone in the bay as the sun goes down, not a ripple disturbs the mercurial water until we break the spell, diving through its surface for an evening swim.

Return to Symi

It had been some 28 years since I had last visited Symi, and my memory of that trip had made me determined to return. Sometimes it takes courage to revisit a place after such a time, especially when it has engraved such a perfect picture in the mind's eye. On that last visit we had been lucky enough to visit the island on our own terms. We had sailed there aboard a beautiful classic carvel-built Bermudan sloop owned by some friends who lived aboard in Mandraki harbour. This time afforded no such luxury; we had to seek passage aboard one of the many tourist boats that now sailed from that same harbour. An easy task you'd have thought, and so did we. We strolled along the bustling quay, passing the fishing boats, bareboat charter hires and polished gin palaces to the moorings where a mish-mash of craft lay at rest, stern on to the sea wall, in serene contrast to their crews touting for business from passing trade.

We stopped astern of one such boat, a sturdy caique with planked, caulked decks and varnished topsides and the ubiquitous white hull with blue trimmings. Its crew hosed down the decks and carried crates of Coke and beer aboard to the rhythm of Lady GaGa playing through the wheelhouse sound system. A man sitting at a folding table, under an umbrella advertising Alpha beer, stopped flicking his worry beads to assure us his was the best boat, at the best price for Symi the next day, just as we wanted.

The price was good, and lower than expected, but that was not unusual in our experience on the island in these cash-strapped times. The next day was a Sunday, yet our new friend was insistent that we arrive at the jetty no later than 8.00am and ask for him, and him alone, 'only ask for Michaelis' he regaled us. 'And don't be late', he insisted with an unusual emphasis on punctuality. I assured him we'd be there, and he wrote us out a receipt as I parted with the cash.

At the time we were staying in Lindos, and thought an hour for the journey to Rhodes Town the next day would be plenty of time, and it would have been, had I learned to master the alarm on my mobile phone. We were left with a mad dash through the breaking dawn avoiding early starters weaving their way to work on bikes. We had no problem parking at that time and arrived on the quay with minutes to spare. Michaelis had not materialised, so we sat down on a bench to wait. Time ticked on, and for someone who had been so insistent that we were punctual, Michaelis was a little tardy.

After waiting twenty minutes, the cabin door on the caique moored next to us opened. Yawning, a crewmember emerged on deck, putting a cup of coffee down on the cockpit table and stretching. He appeared to have the demeanour of a man who was going nowhere soon, so I asked him what time we were leaving for Symi. I think I knew the answer before he replied. It was Sunday and his boat was not going anywhere today. I asked which boat was going and he said he didn't know, and what's more had never heard of Michaelis who had been selling tickets for the trip beside his boat.

At that moment a screeching of tyres announced the arrival of said Michaelis. He leaped out of the most decrepit, tiny, car I had ever seen and started berating me for talking to the man on the boat. The fact he was half an hour late and that no boat was going to our island destination seemed to escape him.

'You must come with me', he said, bundling us into the back seat through the driver's door, the only one apparently that opened. He let the clutch out and the car jumped forward – and stalled. He turned the key and we caught the last deathly gasp of a dying battery. 'This has never happened before', he shouted, although I was surprised the car had not been consigned to the scrap heap some decades ago. He jumped out onto the quay and summoned the crewmember from the caique, along with a couple of passing pedestrians, and inveigled them to push. Michaelis released the clutch with aplomb, for a novice, and the car spluttered into life.

As if afraid to take his foot off the gas, he ploughed through red lights as we sped south along the coast road. 'Today we go from the big ship harbour,' he informed us as we left picturesque Mandraki where our car was parked behind, travelling past the ancient city walls on our right to the more industrial setting of the town's outskirts.

We turned through some gates onto a dusty path in a boatyard where cruisers, yachts, fishing boats and other sundry craft stood beached on trailers, blocked up or propped in various stages of disrepair awaiting the attentions of the boatyard staff.

Through another set of gates we entered an empty car park beside a quay to which was moored a lone, workmanlike, if a little lacklustre, vessel, *Proteus*. We were deposited with undue haste some yards from the craft, which puffed and panted as it idled on its isolated mooring. 'This is your boat', shouted Michaelis, as he sped off leaving us bemused. I had a bad feeling about this, the day was not shaping up to be a sun-kissed voyage on a small traditional craft to revisit the island of our dreams. Undeterred, I approached the stern of the boat where crew in white uniforms sat on bollards smoking.

It didn't take long to realize that *Proteus* was a car ferry. Such workhorses plied their way between the islands, carrying people, vehicles, food and other cargo, which was the lifeblood of the smaller communities. I proffered my tatty receipt to one of the crew, who smiled knowingly and told me I had to go to a small kiosk on the other side of the quay to exchange it for tickets. I did as I was told and traipsed across to the kiosk, which was closed. A notice declared it would open at 10.00 o'clock. Returning to the ship I asked what time they set sail and was told 11.00 o'clock. They left dock later as it was a Sunday.

Proteus was well-named after an ancient God of the oceans, who Homer described as 'The Old Man of the Sea'. Our ship was certainly old, with rusty tears dropping from eyes beneath which hung two hefty anchors. But the boat revealed itself to be truly protean, and our voyage turned out to be all the better for being that of the everyday Greek who visited Symi.

One of the crew took pity on us. He invited us to sit on board until the ticket booth opened, and put out seats for us at the small impromptu café they had set out to the side of the car deck. Here, among boxes of tomatoes, crates of water and shrink-wrapped toilet rolls, their urn bubbled away and we were given coffee and a plate of sweet white grapes to sustain us. At 10.00 o'clock one of our new friends insisted on going and collecting our tickets, and on his return we were ushered upstairs to the saloon of the ship, with its comfortable chairs and tables, a bar selling drinks and snacks and multiple TV sets all tuned in to an animated post-election debate.

As the time ticked on towards 11.00 o'clock the room started to fill up. A party of children with teachers on a day trip to the Monastery of the Archangel Michael at Panormitis Bay; an elderly couple with a minute Chihuahua, its head poking out of a Burberry handbag; workers on a pilgrimage with men looking uncomfortable in Sunday suits, their wives in large patterned floral frocks; an eccentric, chanting lists of English football teams as he searched bins for discarded food before being given a meal by the galley staff; a cross section of Greek life was aboard and we were the only foreigners.

The thudding of the engines grew louder and the deck floor began to vibrate as the lines were cast off and we headed out to sea. As soon as we edged out of the harbour mouth the swell took hold of the vessel, rhythmically pitching and twisting us as we progressed towards the northern cape of the island, before steering a northwesterly course leaving Rhodes behind.

Proteus felt at home in this significant swell but, as the cloud came lower and the sky darkened bringing with it more than a hint of a breeze, I began to be thankful we were aboard this Trojan vessel. As the coast of Turkey loomed ahead the wind abated and the rain began to fall almost vertically from the sky.

Our approach to Panormitis was in sharp contrast to that which we had made all those years ago by yacht. The unrelenting rainfall made the bay look smaller, as we inched towards the jetty beneath the monastery. Crewmen shouted instructions at each other to make themselves heard over the reverse thrust of the ship's engines and the excited chatter of the schoolchildren.

Hawsers were heaved ashore and secured around hefty bollards as the ship's ramp was lowered and we and the other passengers poured ashore. The monastery still retained an undoubted air of grandeur, but with the rain dripping down its walls and polishing the chessboard marble stones of the courtyard, it held us in a melancholy thrall.

Water dripped off the leaves of the potted chrysanthemums, off the brims of hats and hoods and down the backs of shirts. Unabated, the children ran hither and thither between the buildings, while the devout leafed through their guidebooks whispering to each other. We struggled to relive the memory of our first visit, inwardly disappointed that the weather did not allow this magnificent spot to give off its best.

If the rain had presented us with a clammy, uncomfortable feeling, and lacklustre picture for the eyes, it was compensated for by the aroma the soaking had released from the hills behind the monastery. Wild arugula, sage, thyme and selino made their presence felt as the rain subsided and the ground began to steam in the watery sunlight. The smell of herbs aroused the taste buds and we had to be strong to resist sitting down to eat, which we intended to do in Symi Town, our next port of call.

As *Proteus* edged out of the bay, leaving the small village behind, the sun began to dry us out and projected a beautiful rainbow arching from the sea over the monastery to the mountainside beyond. Making short work of burning off the mist and cloud, the sun reestablished its dominance almost as sharply as it had previously been undermined. We settled down hugging the shore bound for Symi Town. Buffeting a slight swell we eased our way to the southern tip of the coastline before skirting around the small island of Sesklia, its stark landscape inhabited only by seabirds, including pink-footed shearwaters. At times seals languish here, but today they were hiding. This is part of the coast that made Symi famous and was the source of much of its wealth in the past.

The steep shelving rocks which dive into the sea were the ideal place for sponges to grow and the local population were second to none in their skill and bravery in harvesting these natural wonders. Since the time of Homer their renown had been widespread in the eastern Mediterranean and, apart from the direct riches diving for sponges brought to the island, it also endowed the people with a unique bargaining power, which they used to good effect when threatened by the expanding territorial ambitions of the Ottoman Empire in the 16th Century.

The pragmatic islanders sent representatives to the sultan, Suleiman the Magnificent. They proffered gifts of their best sponges and promises that, if allowed to trade freely in both sponges and in the fast and sturdy ships their craftsmen constructed, they could be of great use to the Turks – Suleiman assented. They enjoyed such privileges until 1830 when, after the islanders joined the struggle for Greek independence, their rights were curtailed. Prior to this the Symiots enjoyed freedoms unknown in the rest of occupied Greece. For the price of some nominal taxation and a yearly gift of the most extravagant sponges to the Harem of the Sultan's palace in Istanbul, the islanders were allowed to carry on trading much as normal. And trade they did. So much is obvious by the wealth exhibited in the wonderful architecture on display as we enter the protective arms of the natural harbour of Symi Town itself on the north-eastern coast.

The withdrawal of certain privileges by the Turks following the Symiots ill-fated alliance with other Greeks in the 1821 revolution was the beginning of the end for the wealthy sponge merchants and shipwrights. Much of the skill and bravery involved in diving for sponges was superseded with the invention of diving suits. Prior to this the fishermen used to dive naked, being aided to the seabed by a *skandalopetra*. As the '*petra*' in the name might suggest, this was a specially-shaped stone weighing around 30lbs, which was perforated to reduce water resistance. The stone would be tied to the diver with twine and by a rope to a boat on the surface. Holding on to the rock the fisherman would quickly descend to as deep as 100 feet below the surface where, for up to four minutes he would harvest sponges before cutting himself free from the stone and returning to the surface. The crew of the boat then hauled up his *skandalopetra*. The danger and skill involved made the sponges an expensive luxury, but the advent of more sophisticated sub-aqua equipment meant that sponges rapidly became over fished and fishermen had to go deeper and deeper to find them. This in turn hastened the end of the trade. Many divers died due to their ignorance of the effect of water pressure on the human body and the resultant bends inflicted by resurfacing too quickly.

Honey, sand and terracotta pastel shades unveil themselves through the rain-rinsed skies as this gem of a town reveals itself, stepping backwards up the steep hills and making an amphitheatre around the long, narrow harbour. The buildings are mostly neo-classical, built in the 18th and early 19th Centuries, the heyday of Symi's trading, when their access to the vast Ottoman markets made merchants rich beyond imagination. The town's beauty is a legacy of a life no longer sustainable, and today the small local community survives mostly from the earnings from tourism.

Disembarking, our spirits lifted by the sunshine, it didn't take long to find a suitable taverna where plenty of Greeks were sitting down to tuck into their family Sunday lunch. I settled down to bread dipped in oil and vinegar with a black olive paste. This was followed by grilled mackerel, its tiger stripes burnished with lemon juice and crackling sea salt, served with a ramekin of mustard sauce glistening with the freshness of golden eggs, vinegar, mustard and butter and heavily scented with sage and thyme. The white wine was chilled to within an inch of its life. Served in a copper jug, echoing the steely edge of the wine itself, it cut through the oiliness of my fish as though every individual grape used in its making had been grown just for that moment. It would have been easy to idle away the remaining couple of hours just sitting there in that waterfront taverna, maybe eating an ice cream or indulging in another carafe of wine. But the narrow streets that led away from the harbour were beckoning and overcame any more sybaritic intentions we may have held. We paid our bill, and reluctantly brought ourselves up to ambling pace and headed away from the quayside.

The town is split into two areas. The low-lying port, Yialos, and the old town of Horio that looks down on it from the hills to the south. Just away from the bustling southwest corner of the harbourside is a flight of about 400 steps. These connect the low-lying commercial centre of Yialos with the older settlement of Horio, and replaced the older kataraktis footpath, which runs up to the ancient acropolis. This was the preferred way up the hillside until the kali strata steps were laid in the 19th Century.

The houses that line the route are imposing. Some have seen better days, their flakey exteriors disguising their past grandeur. They stand testament to the halcyon days when the island's wealth from sponges, shipbuilding and wine production supported a lifestyle that was the envy of other islands in the Dodecanese. But the town's history can be traced back much further.

The island is said to have been named after Syme who, according to the 2nd-century AD rhetorician, Athenaeus, was the daughter of Ialyssos, the King of Rhodes, and Dotis. The sea god, Glaucus, a fisherman who, if Ovid is to be believed, achieved deity by eating a magical herb, abducted the poor girl. He brought her to the deserted island, which then took her name. Glaucus himself was imbued with many of the skills that the island later became famous for, being one of the shipwrights who built Jason's ship, the *Argo*. As a god, he swam in the waters surrounding the island, ensuring safe passage for sailors and rescuing fishermen in distress.

Homer wrote that three ships sailed from Symi to join the Greek fleet at Troy and the island's king Nereus, who commanded these ships, perished in the campaign. The subsequent history of the island is inextricably linked to Rhodes itself, Symi being a satellite held by the comings and goings of the powers on the larger island. The Dorians, followed by the Romans, held sway here before the island became part of the Byzantine Empire.

The climb up the kali strata is steep and every step moves us further back in time. Small pathways feeling their ways between lime-washed and pastel-coloured homes, blue doors open and matching shutters closed in the afternoon sun. The Knights of St John built a castle on the top of the acropolis on the site of a Byzantine citadel, which had also taken advantage of this site with its magnificent views of the harbour.

The medieval fortress remained intact until the last century, when it was used as a munitions dump by the occupying German forces during the Second World War. When they realized the game was up, the retreating troops blew up their stashpile, destroying most of the castle, surrounding homes and the Church of the Assumption that was enclosed within the walls of the fortress. The remnants of the castle walls are all that is left, but a new church has risen on the hill to replace that destroyed by the Germans. Each

Sunday as its bells ring, one of those that tolls serves as a reminder of those dark days, as it is forged from the nose of a massive German bomb.

Back on the north side of the harbour front, where *Proteus* was readying herself for departure, is a place that serves as a reminder of those times. What is now the Hotel Les Katarinettes was formerly the Kampsopoulou Mansion where, on the 8th of May 1945, the Germans made their formal surrender of the Dodecanese to the Allies. Nearby is a war memorial hewn out of the mountainside. Its inscription reads: 'On this day freedom whispered to me. "You twelve islands, no longer be downhearted".'

Sailing out through the headlands of the bay, we stood on deck enjoying the breeze created by the ship making its way south again. As evening draws in the island will turn back in on itself, its population of little more than 2,000 reclaiming their tranquillity. We watched from the stern deck as Symi fell slowly under the shadow of the Turkish coast, and we headed back to Rhodes. A chilled sweet Samos Muscat wine from our cool bag made the perfect accompaniment to a pile of Loukoumades coated in honey and dusted lightly with cinnamon to see us through until dinner time.

Icons – Prayers Made Visible

Something that set Greece aside from anywhere I had ever visited before was the profusion of dimly lit, cavernous shops selling icons. In the back of these studios artists sat, hunched over easels creating works of art in a style with which I was to become familiar. Although the profusion of these studios is no longer so apparent, every town has a shop selling these religious works. It seemed strange to me that such art so often seemed to be created in darkness, unlike the paintings and sculptures of Western artists which celebrate the light. But having learned more about these religious works I now understand that the light is not required as these are not likenesses of worldly things or representations of the artist's imagination, but they are prayers made visible. *Eikon* in Greek means image, and just as Christians believe that Christ was created in the image of God, these representations of religious figures are analogous rather than realistic.

On chapel walls, in private homes, on church iconostasis throughout Greece these radiant gateways to the Lord can be seen in all their stylised splendour. Rumour has it that the first physical records of icons relate to pre-Christian times, to when Roman Emperors were venerated as divine beings and pictures of them were displayed around the empire for people to display their obeisance by burning candles and scented oils in their presence. Indeed, it is this link to the pagan past that throughout history has created rifts in the church about the veneration of images. Some faiths allude to the Old Testament view that such things went against the commandment of making 'graven images'. In fact the flattened nature of the work traditionally goes back to the belief that in three-dimensional, realistic sculptures lurked demons with supernatural powers, not unlike those powers held by the gods of Greek legend. Icons in the Greek Orthodox faith are usually portrayed on flat panels. If they are ever sculpted or carved, icons will always be less obtrusive than bas relief and as such will have considerably less depth to the figures than they would have if they were proportionately to scale.

Here icons are a constant presence in daily life, they hang in corners in the poorest of homes, adorn the walls of the most inaccessible chapels on mountain tops, emblazon the iconostasis of city cathedrals or comfort the loved ones of those killed in accidents in roadside shrines. But all these religious works, whether they are in the simplest of forms or 'drawn' by a grand master hold one thing in common, they all adhere to a strict set of conventions.

Christ and the saints are always represented with halos, as are angels who are also adorned with wings, as they are the messengers of God. This symbolism accounts for a style that is self-consciously the antithesis of realism. Golden backgrounds represent the incandescence of heaven, blue is used to colour humans while red illustrates beatific divinity. A stylized letter convention is also incorporated to help identify the scene and the characters that enact it.

These conventions not only serve to take the icon out of the temporal world of human reality, but also act as a code which could be understood by even the least literate members of society. They became a direct way for an uneducated society to learn the gospels; indeed icons were used as a way of converting people to the faith after the declaration of religious tolerance following the conversion of the Roman Emperor Constantine the Great himself in 313 AD. They were a *lingua franca* that could be exploited, as the iconic form had been used from the earliest of times for the veneration of ancient gods and former Roman emperors themselves. The most famous of the Greek Orthodox Schools of iconography was based in Heraklion in Crete. By the 16th Century this was an established centre for post-Byzantine art, and El Greco was a Master of this renowned painters' guild before leaving Greece to work in Venice and Spain. But Rhodes has some outstanding representations of the icon painter's art, examples of which can be found in two churches on the island, that of the Assumption of Our Lady in the narrow lanes of Lindos and the more remote but no less meritorious Church of the Dormition of the Virgin in Asklipio. But similar work is to be viewed across Rhodes and sometimes in the most unlikely of places. Wherever it turns up, it is always a joy.

Monolithos – A Fairy-tale Castle

I don't know why I had not heard about Monolithos before actually stumbling upon it on a drive around the south west of Rhodes. It is sublimely peaceful, and is none the worse for hiding its light under the proverbial bushel. The first reason we stopped there was hunger. Every day I try not to eat a sizeable lunch in an attempt to preserve my appetite for dinner, and on this particular day I failed spectacularly. Driving up from the southernmost tip of the island one Sunday, the road from Prasonissi Cape and Apolakkia happens upon an unpretentious gem of a restaurant. Sited at the point where the road arrives at the outskirts of Monolithos before heading northwards, playing hide and seek with Rhodes' spectacular western seaboard a third road peels off and heads into the village itself. At this meeting of the ways stands Christos' Corner Taverna.

As the first lunchtime customers, we had the pick of the outside tables. Not long afterwards a string of locals were arriving. Soon all the tables, in a no doubt prescient way, were full to busting. Christos led us to his kitchen, if that's what you can call a large fridge next to a charcoal grill beneath a flimsy shelter in the middle of the jumble of tables. This was where most of the cooking was done, and he proudly showed us what was on offer. Any hope of having a light lunch was extinguished in the face of a mouth-watering display of refrigerated souvlaki, chicken, chops, and numerous fish.

The smoke from the recently-lit grill gave off an enticing aroma of herbs from previously cooked delights and all resolve was abandoned. I ordered pork chops and a Greek salad. When it arrived at the table I was left wondering from which behemoth of an unfortunate pig these cuts had been butchered. Two succulent, giant chops overlapped the sides of my plate barely leaving room for two foil-wrapped jacket potatoes. A roughly hewn loaf of bread was squeezed onto the table between two enormous salads, a bowl of fresh tzatziki and an earthenware jug of red wine. The creamy potatoes dripping with butter and the melting chunks of meat brushed with oil and all manner of herbs from the surrounding hills made the challenge of eating such a quantity all too achievable.

Having finished and requesting the bill we were brought glasses of a clear spirit called souma. This is made locally, and is a distillation of dried figs. Slightly sweet and strong, it has a taste distinctive from its better-known cousins Raki and Ouzo, but its capacity to slow down the system is much the same. Not wanting to waste the rest of the day sleeping in the sun, we headed for the village centre.

From the tranquil air that pervades this small place it is clear this must be a well-kept secret. There is little to do here except inhale the beauty and atmosphere, which I consider one of the most perfect spots on the island. Beyond the classic white houses, their courtyards ablaze with the ubiquitous bougainvillea and geraniums, lies the sea, sanguine beneath the towering cliffs dominated by a dazzling outcrop on which languish the remains of the striking castle for which the village is famous. The isolation is reminiscent of King Arthur's legendary fortress at Tintagel in Cornwall, but this redoubt was more recent, built by the Knights of St John in 1480 to protect from invaders and pirates.

What is left of the castle stands upon the rock that gives this charmed spot its name *mono lithos*, meaning 'lonely rock'. It can be reached by way of a narrow, steep staircase hewn out of the cliff face. Parking at the bottom of the crag we began the trek upwards. A lighter lunch might have been sensible, but the breathless hike to the top is worth it, not least to take a look around the ruined walls that encircle the remains of two small chapels and the cisterns, which would have provided for the basic needs of the garrison stationed here. The real reward for the climb, however, is the view. Beneath the vertiginous, 300-foot cliffs tiny, secluded beaches burrow into their secret coves. Out to sea, peeking through the heat-haze of breathless air, are two small islands moored offshore, and inland a lush pine forest floods the foothills of Rhodes' second highest peak. Mount Akramytis rises some 2700 feet above the tiny village glimpsed beneath us inland. The forest is so different from much of the landscape elsewhere on the island. It comes as a shock after the barrenness of the south from where we have just come.

We return to the car and drive back to the outskirts of the village and stop to buy from one of the many honey sellers who have set up shop alongside the winding road. The woman is proud of her produce, telling me it comes from her brother's hives that sit in the vast acreage of pine forest. She lets me taste the different honeys on offer, explaining the provenance of each batch. Savouring them together, the difference in flavour was incredible.

The pine honey was especially surprising as I was tasting something redolent of Christmas, sweet but infused with the taste of the trees from which the bees reap their harvest. Darker and thicker than the other honey on display, its heaviness chimed more readily with this image of wintertime. But the bees' harvest is not directly from the trees themselves but from honey dew, which is a sugary secretion deposited on the trees by insects that live off sap from the pine. In the heat of a Rhodian afternoon, in that brazen sunshine overlooking the most sedate of cerulean seas, the taste of that honey was endowed with a purity that seemed only achievable when a food is enjoyed in its natural environment.

It was intriguing to experience the difference between the varieties of honey deriving from a range of plants and herbs. The thyme honey was a natural antioxidant, so the stallholder told me, and others had the scent and taste of wild oregano and rosemary. I bought more than enough to enjoy with my breakfast yoghurts throughout my stay.

We were right on the verge of the pine forest. Instead of heading back to the village we took a detour along a road that delved into the trees. The air cooled under the shade of the fronds of the thousands of pines, which stretched for miles inland. In clearings stood stacks of felled trunks awaiting their journey to the sawmill. Everywhere dotted among the vast evergreens, resting on a carpet of cones, seeds and needles were multicoloured hives. I have never seen more beehives in Greece, or anywhere else for that matter. The air hangs limpid in the forest, the silence only broken by the odd worker bee going about its business in the heat of the afternoon, most of their co-workers perhaps taking the wise course of action and indulging in an afternoon snooze. After driving for several miles, the road became a track, which gradually got more rutted and threatened to overwhelm our tiny hire car. We retraced our steps leaving the forest behind, emerging once more into the full strength of the light reflecting off the sea some hundreds of feet below our meagre road that desperately clung to the sheer cliff.

Feta – A Taste of Victory

Membership of the EC may be a contentious issue in Greece these days, but one thing the Greeks will always be grateful to the Brussels' bureaucrats for is their landmark ruling in 2005 giving protected designation of origin (PDO) status to that cheese which crowns the ubiquitous Greek salad, feta. No longer can inferior grade products be passed off as the cheese that lies at the heart of so much of Greece's cuisine. Not only does this crumbly, tangy, brined cheese with an unmistakable aroma of the ewe's milk, so essential to its authenticity, glisten with golden oil as it crowns horiatiki salata it is also a key ingredient in so many other Greek staples. Its use in tyropita, small filo pastry parcels stuffed with cheese, omelettes and a wealth of saganaki dishes, to name but a few, contribute to making the Greeks the biggest consumers of cheese in Europe.

The battle over the right to call a cheese feta was fierce, the main protagonists surprisingly being northern European countries in the form of Denmark and Germany. Both these countries produced large quantities of soft, brined cheeses made from cow's milk. The Danes were the Greek's largest competitors producing some 25,000 tonnes for export with the Germans manufacturing a not insubstantial 20,000 tonnes. The Danes started to make the cheese in the 1930s and the Germans as late as the 1970s although they only jumped on the bandwagon and marketed their versions of the cheese as 'feta' in 1963 and 1985 respectively.

Feta is the Greek word for slice. Whether this refers to the way the cheese is sliced on top of salads of how the cheese is cut up to be put into the wooden barrels in which it is traditionally matured has been lost in the sands of time as the cheese has been referred to by its current name since the 17th Century. Greek claims to the cheese go back even further than that. An Italian traveller to Crete wrote of seeing such a cheese being cured in baths of brine as early as 1494. Being of Byzantine origin it would clearly see off the foreign interlopers, but legend has it that such cheese dates back some 2000 years earlier still, the museum at Delphi exhibiting artefacts from early cheese making from the 6th Century BC.

The battle raged from 1996 when the EC first gave protection to feta, the name only being allowed to be used for cheeses produced in certain parts of Greece and made from a minimum of 70 per cent sheep's milk the other percentage being goats' milk. It was also ruled that the cheese must be made using certain traditional methods. Challenges from other countries were not finally fought off until 2005 when the EC's highest court, the European Court of Justice eventually ruled in Greece's favour.

For lovers of this sublime cheese which, at its best, combines a creamy texture while remaining crumbly, and a salty taste which still has hints of sweetness coming through, this was the right decision. The best feta has been matured in wooden barrels. It feeds off its own juices for weeks before being stored for months more, maturing until ready to eat. For real connoisseurs I am told the best time to eat the cheese is July, as feta bought straight from the barrel at this time will have been made from the milk of ewes which grazed on the best of the new spring herbs and grasses, imbuing the cheese with the scents and flavours of the hillside.

The cheese is made by heating pure sheep's milk or a blend of sheep and goats' milk in a vat before rennet is added to induce the separation of curds and whey. The curds are then cut into small pieces before being put into perforated moulds and left for more of the whey to drain off. Sprinkled with salt and left overnight for this to absorb the curds are then cut into pieces and squeezed into wooden barrels where they sit in any more whey which has been expelled.

After several days the barrel is sealed tightly, any air inside is pumped out so the cheese is in a vacuum where it remains for up to 20 days fermenting on its own yeast and bacteria. After this time the barrels almost explode open at which point they are checked for taste before water is added and the barrels are resealed and refrigerated for three months or more. At that stage the cheese is ready for market.

This is an age-old process that has changed little over the years and the end product is a world away from the bland thin, watery cheeses masquerading as feta and often marked 'Greek style' in supermarkets outside Greece. Nothing is wasted in the traditional manufacture of feta. The small pieces of cheese that are produced when it is sliced are called *trimma* (crumble). This is often given away and ideal for using in cheese pies or sprinkling into an omelette or on a chunk of oiled bread and herbs. Even the separated whey does not go to waste. It is blended with skimmed milk and heated up again with rennet and formed into a hard cheese which, after aging for more than a year, is perfect for grating over dishes. It is possible to make something resembling this cheese at home, just as long as you remember not to call it feta…

Greece's Day of Pride

If any colours can be said to represent Greece they are blue and white. Brightly painted blue shutters and doors are features on the faces of the brilliant white buildings that glisten in the sun across the whole of the nation. Blue eyes stare out of the white hulls of the fishing caiques that bob up and down at anchor in a thousand harbours and bays around its coasts. Most days in spring, summer and autumn the bluest of blue seas meets a white sky bleached by the fierce midday sun.

On one day in particular, the blue and white is even more in evidence than usual. On October 28th each year, the blue and white flag of Greece flutters from every available pole, mast or makeshift halyard across the nation. It flutters in remembrance of a noble nation's clear act of defiance, standing up against the Axis powers in World War Two, despite the devastating consequences.

Although Rhodes had yet to be united into the new Greece and became embroiled in the war by default as it was already under Italian occupation the island still celebrates this pivotal moment in history. Already in the possession of the Italians, Rhodes and the rest of the Dodecanese archipelago were put on a war footing, which marked an immediate downturn in their fortunes.

The day is a national holiday and is celebrated with parades, feasting and dancing to mark one of modern Greece's finest hours. More than any other moment in Greek history this day epitomizes their belief in the battle cry from the War of Independence against the Ottoman Turks in the 1820s, *elefteria i thanatos*, 'freedom or death'. Ochi Day quite literally means 'No Day', and marks the succinct reply given by Greek Prime Minister Ioannis Metaxas in response to an ultimatum from the Italian fascist dictator Benito Mussolini in 1940.

Following a party at the German Embassy in Athens, the Italian Ambassador to Greece, Emanuele Grazzi, approached Metaxas with Mussolini's demand that Greece should permit Axis forces to enter the country and take up whatever strategic positions they saw fit or face war.

The Prime Minister answered with the one word, '*ochi*'', that moment is now celebrated on October 28th each year. This was the start of Greece's bloody involvement in the Second World War. Within one and a half hours of this refusal to cooperate, Italian troops were streaming over the border into Greece from bases in Italian occupied Albania.

The Italians, although vastly outnumbering the Greeks and having much superior firepower, were pushed back across the border in a humiliating defeat that many believe proved decisive in the final outcome of the war. Hitler was forced to commit large numbers of German forces to assist the Italians, and in so doing critically delayed his invasion of Russia, resulting in his troops having to fight on that front during the Soviet winter.

Although Greece succumbed to the military might of Germany, there was fierce resistance to the invaders that kept vast enemy resources occupied until mainland Greece was finally liberated in 1944.

Whether it is apocryphal or not, I would like to believe that it is true, as is claimed by many Greeks, that the nine blue and white stripes on the Greek flag symbolize the number of syllables in those three words *elefteria i thanatos* which so embodies the spirit of its people. How appropriate it is that this proud country is awash with blue and white flags on this special day.

A Journey Back in Time – Palia Poli

Ten gates punctuate the sturdy walls of the Palia Poli, or Rhodes Old Town. To pass through any of them is to enter into another world. Within the two and a half miles of fortifications built by the Knights Hospitaller on top of earlier Byzantine defences lies an intriguing snapshot from which the inquisitive visitor can glean much of the island's turbulent past. The whole of the old town is a World Heritage Site, designated as such by UNESCO in 1988 and, spending any amount of time meandering within the walls of this medieval fortress town, it is easy to see why.

Cultural edifices from Hellenistic, Roman, Byzantine, Medieval, Ottoman and Italian periods of the town's history are all represented here. Those who seek evidence of the earlier heritage of Rhodes will need to go further afield, to the ancient capitals of Lindos, Ialyssos or Kamiros which held sway until a pact between their leaders paved the way for the creation of the original Palia Poli in 408 BC.

For most though there is plenty to satisfy here, and the architectural style which pervades at first would appear to be that of the Knights. But some of this is pastiche, the work of heavy-handed Italian ideologues trying to create a long forgotten chivalric era in the image of the crusaders. The Italian influence came crashing down under the marching heels of the jackboots of their erstwhile allies the Germans in 1943 an echo of the eventual capitulation of the Knights some four hundred years earlier to the Ottoman forces of Suleiman the Magnificent in 1522.

The folly of that ill-conceived Italian dynasty may have restructured parts of the town in a cold, stern idealisation of what they held to be medieval, but things could have been so much worse. To the untrained eye the flying buttressed lanes of the original city segue effortlessly into the reconstructed facsimile and in passing it is difficult to see the joins.

Nowhere more is this true than in the Anaktoro ton Arkhonton, the Palace of the Grand Masters. This lies at the heart of the higher part of the city, to the north west, the Knights themselves constructing their castle, the Collachium, on earlier Byzantine fortifications. The Palace was the epicentre of Hospitaller governance, housing the offices of state and the most senior denizens of their chivalric society. Outside of the Collachium lies the Hora, where the working population of the city lived and went about their business.

The Palace sits on the Ippoton, the aptly named Street of the Knights, which has a pleasing sense of relaxed splendour befitting its heritage. This is maintained by the absence of shops and restaurants along its length. In these reconstructed buildings, which have been set aside by the great and the good of the modern administration to house administrative and cultural offices, used to reside the Knights.

For the Hospitallers, Rhodes was the safe haven they had been seeking after centuries of conflict. The Order can be traced back to 1048. It was then that it was founded in Jerusalem to administer to the needs of pilgrims visiting the city. As tensions rose with the crusades, the Knights of Saint John succumbed to the militarisation of their number and were charged by the church to defend the Holy Sepulchre in Jerusalem to their last breath. Evicted from the city by Saladin in 1191 they wandered the region before settling in western Galilee in the city of Acre before fleeing to Cyprus in the face of Mamluk forces in 1291. Infighting between The Hospitallers and the incumbent Knights Templar led to the order being driven off that island in 1306 when, desperate for a new home, they attacked the Byzantine fiefdom of Rhodes, prevailing in 1309 after a protracted siege.

In the ground floors of these buildings on the Ippoton where clerks now sit drinking coffee and idling over spreadsheets, horses used to be shod, fed and watered as squires and farriers tended to the needs of their master's mount and armoury while, in the chambers above, the Knights would make plans to exploit the wealth of, and defend, their newfound home.

Members of the Order came from all over the Christian world, and were divided into units called Tongues, dependent on their nationality. From Spain, Italy, Germany, England, Provence, The Auvergne and the rest of France, Knights joined this new order that had found favour and support from the papacy. Along this street can be found, among others, the turreted and gargoyled Inn of the Tongue of France. Like the other groupings of Knights this enclave would be presided over by a bailiff and the Knights would elect a leader for life from their number who became the Grand Master. The original palace built by the Knights survived the siege of Sulieman which ousted them from the city in 1522, but failed to weather an accidental explosion when it was being used as an ammunitions dump by the Turks in 1856. The cool, sand-coloured lines of the present incarnation of the building is an Italian architect's interpretation of the original, brought to fruition in the 1930s.

The palace encloses a beautiful arched and cloistered courtyard, and houses two museum collections, one of Rhodian artefacts and another specifically medieval. Elsewhere the exhibits are more eclectic. Climbing the grand staircase to the upper chambers that look out across the inlaid grey and yellow squares of the inner sanctum there are mosaic floors from both Hellenistic and Roman periods, incongruously laid down in this 20th-century homage to the medieval. But it would be churlish not to acknowledge the magnificence of this building, whatever its dubious heritage, which in a way encapsulates a wider pantheon of Rhodian history than it might have done if it had remained neglected.

The Hora is less grand but more authentic and serendipitous, the streets of sandstone and lime-washed buildings with iron-fortified windows and blazing blue doors weave their cobbled ways between hidden chochlakia (pebbled) courtyards, tiny cracked churches and crumbling mosques. A snatch of modern Europop emanating from an open window can do little to break the reverie this magical place engenders, a hotch-potch of Gothic, Turkish, Byzantine buildings buttressed against potential earthquake as they meander from shaded square to hidden residences resplendent with summer blooms. On Sokratous Street the old rubs shoulders with the new. Traders and restaurateurs lucky enough to own a slice of this popular piece of history go about their business, catering to the needs of the thousands of tourists who prefer the hustle and bustle of this one deeply flowing street and its tributaries.

I have often been pleasantly surprised at how it is still possible to find an authentic and reasonably priced meal right here in the centre of Rhodes' cultural heartland. There are few other places embued with such an atmosphere where you can enjoy watching the world go by to an accompaniment of a plate of flash fried kalimari with lemon juice.

Lost in Lindos

Picture perfect, Lindos is the epitome of the classic Greek island town. So much so that in recent years it has carved out a niche for itself as a popular wedding destination. The labyrinthine lanes weaving their way between the sturdy, brilliant white walls of family dwellings and shops, and the delights of numerous rooftop restaurants have seduced many an engaged couple. All this in the shadow of the imposing citadel of the acropolis which tops the spectacular spur of rock which has stood guard over the tiny town for all remembered time.

Heavy bare-wood doors, dressed in uncompromising black ironmongery, stand open to reveal the mosaic chochlakia floors of a thousand courtyards. These intricately laid black and white beach pebbles set in symmetrical shapes which allude to Lindos' maritime past or even just to the aesthetic whim of a master craftsman are said to massage the bare-footed stroller in much the same way as pressure points in acupuncture or chiropody. Whether this is true or not, they provide a striking location for families to eat, drink and siesta as cats doze in the shade of potted pink, purple, red and yellow hibiscus, barely opening one eye to the swallows busying themselves building nests in the gnarled old beams above.

Had I not glimpsed these delights for myself some years earlier, I would have been unaware of what awaited me, as a twelve hour delay in our flight from the UK had left us struggling to find our accommodation at three o'clock in the morning, with little idea where we were going. A little apartment hiding in the old town, away from the bustle of the centre but within easy reach of its attractions is to be highly recommended, if you can find it in the first place. With the streets deserted and some rather inexact directions this turned into something of a mission. After toying with us for long enough for us to consider returning to the car and awaiting sunrise, the gods of the maze revealed our accommodation. We stumbled over the threshold, across the courtyard sweeping aside fronds of potted palms that brushed our faces before we tumbled into bed.

I was awoken by the clamour of bells, that had scant regard for the sleep of exhausted travellers, the wavelength of which stirred the old walls of our flat like a burgeoning earthquake. Flinging open the shutters, the sound came flooding in on the coat tails of the brilliant light that seeped into every nook and cranny, dispelling any annoyance at the untimely reveille. Flattered by its invitation, the delicious sun drew me outside in search of the makings of a simple breakfast; coffee, bread, yoghurt and honey. Foolishly the lessons of the following night had not been learned. Tracking down a shop selling the required provisions was easy but retracing my steps was not so simple. By the time I got back to our rooms, I was more than ready to enjoy the not-so-recently acquired fruits of my labour.

Lindos is built on a spot of supreme natural beauty, and over the years its inhabitants have, for the most part, been in tune with their surroundings, leaving a sympathetic legacy that satisfies on so many different levels. Split into two distinct areas, the lower town is the commercial and residential sector, whereas the upper town, which encompasses the older settlement, is the acropolis built on top of a rock that towers some 400 feet over two natural harbours to the north and south.

It is easy to see how settlers favoured such a location as early as the 12th Century BC, when the Dorian King Tlepolemus decided to put down roots there. Its natural attributes and geographic location far to the east in the Mediterranean made it a natural stopping place where Greeks and Phoenicians could do trade, and it became the most important of the three ancient Dorian cities on the island. Until 408 BC these three great centres of Ialyssos, Kamiros and Lindos, competed for trade until the elders took the unusually pragmatic approach to combine their resources, revoke their independence and build a new city – that of Rhodes Town. This unification was called the synoecism, but although government moved to the new city of Rhodes, Lindos remained an important religious focal point and important seaport with her own colonies as far away as Asia Minor and Sicily.

As the temple celebrating the cult of Athena Lindia, built as long ago as the 10th Century BC, attests, this site has been one of profound religious significance since the earliest of times. The original Doric temple was probably erected in celebration of the local ancient cult of the goddess of Lindos sharing devotions with the Dorian goddess Athena, which settlers brought with them from overseas and assimilated with the existing local beliefs. What can be seen today, however, was built in the 4th Century BC around a new temple constructed there following the destruction of the original building by fire in 392 BC.

Just as they have been for the past 30 centuries, people are still drawn to the summit of this sheer promontory. The ascent is not for the faint hearted as the stairs rise steeply enough to catch the breath; although an alternative of taking a donkey ride to the summit is a possibility. As a rule I shy away from such things as I have been to some places in Greece where I have been concerned for the animals' welfare.

Having said this the 'Lindos taxis', as these working donkeys are affectionately known, do seem to be well cared for. Their ancestors no doubt have plied this route hauling goods, building materials and travellers for a succession of Greeks, Romans, Byzantines, Knights of St John, Turks and Italians, all of which have left their mark on the plateau at the summit of this outcrop.

Legend has it that the founder of this blessed place was the eponymous Lindos, a grandson of the sun god Helios. Others hold that Danaus, the first leader of all the Hellenic peoples, was first to step foot here en route from Egypt to Ancient Greece, naming Lindos after one of his three daughters, before going on to found Ialyssos and Kamiros, named after the other two girls – all three of his offspring were worshipped as goddesses. The Greek poet and chronicler Homer talks of these three cities being founded by the Dorians and of how Lindos under King Tleptolemos was a major contributor of ships to the fleet in the Trojan wars of which the king took personal command.

After climbing the medieval steps that ascend from the entrance to the archaeological site, it is worth stopping at the first level where the magnificent carving of a Rhodian warship bears witness to the island's maritime heritage. Although more recent than the Trojan wars, dated around 180 BC, this relief of the stern of a trireme is believed to be the work of the sculptor Pythokritos and formed part of the base to a statue, which an inscription on the ship's side tells us was of Admiral Agesander, son of Mikion.

Staring at the graceful swanlike neck of the aft quarters of this galley it is easy to be transported back to the Peloponnesian War of the 5th Century BC where, as members of the Delian Confederation, Rhodes supplied ships for the Athenian fleet, before swapping allegiances to the victorious Spartans not long before their victory. Three tiers of oarsmen numbering some 160 could propel such ships over 60 miles a day. They were used for ramming the enemy or transporting troops and supplies for land battle. In the true spirit of Athenian democracy of the time, they were not crewed by slaves, but by an assortment of free men either fulfilling their military service or paid hands. The ships would only travel by day and were of light enough construction to be beached by the crew overnight.

Lindos continued this seagoing tradition and its dependency on trade led it to establish shipping laws. These developed through the period of the Roman Empire and became Rhodian Sea Law around 600 BC. During the Byzantine period these became the naval laws that in turn became the basis for modern maritime law dealing with shipping regulations and the responsibilities and liabilities for cargo.

I am standing beside the three underground cisterns which were used since the Hellenistic period for the essential storage of water, reminding me it would be wise to take a drink myself as the early morning heat is already winding itself up to fever pitch. Even at this height, the view out to sea is breathtaking. Some of the boats below announce themselves with the bass tones of their engines singing through the still air while others sail silently, leaving behind a ribbon of white as the only evidence of their passing. I could sit here for hours, but am aware that the tourist traffic up the medieval stairs is already increasing and I am determined to enjoy the acropolis in relative solitute.

Dragging my gaze from the sea I focus on making footfall up the steep and uneven staircase that leads to the Governor's Palace, which is identified by the coat of arms of the ubiquitous Grand Master Pierre d'Aubusson high up on the wall. The leader of the island's ruling Knights of St John was also responsible for the building of the magnificent hospital in Rhodes Town, among other architectural gems, between 1476 and his death in 1503 AD. This building augmented the fortifications and the settlements already established by the Knights, overlaying much of the Hellenistic and Roman remains that had fallen into disrepair prior to their settlement of the island in 1309 AD. Built with its outfacing walls rising from the precipitous cliff side, this naturally impregnable building has been restored and now houses the offices of the archaeological teams dedicated to the ongoing restoration work of the acropolis.

Unlike most of Greece and its islands, it is the Gothic architectural style brought here by the Knights Hospitaller for which Rhodes is perhaps most remembered. It is the inclusion of such architecture into the ecumenical mix of historical buildings that contributes greatly to the island's fascination as a destination. And, as I continue uphill, nowhere is this more in evidence than on the acropolis at Lindos. From the 15th-century medieval archway, the domain of the knights gives way to the remains of a Byzantine church dedicated to St John some two centuries earlier.

Turning right up a stairway I pass what is signed as a storage area from around the 1st Century BC, before entering the stoa. Built in the 2nd Century BC this area was once a large covered walkway, which provided respite from the pounding midday sun. It also provided a dramatic approach to the grandiose great stairway, built on the original ascent, dedicated to the pre-Socratic philosopher king, Cleobolus, who ruled the settlement in the 6th Century BC and was responsible for discovering the underwater springs which provided the water to sustain it. His tomb is on the hillside to the north of Lindos. Cleobolus was one of the Seven Sages of Greek thinkers feted by Plato to whom the words *'meden agan'* (nothing in excess) inscribed in the Temple of Phoebus Apollo at Delphi are attributed.

Today, less than half of the original 42 Doric columns remain, but their surprising resilience is more than enough to paint a picture of the magnificence of the stoa, which pre-empted the ascent to the Temple of Lindia Athena which crowns the plateau at the summit of the hill. The impact of the temple, set to the left of the plateau poised upon a dramatic sheer drop to the sea beneath, belies its relatively small size which, at some 72 feet in length and 26 feet wide, is considerably smaller than that of the stoa below. Built in the 4th Century BC, what can be seen today replaced a previous older place of worship, which was destroyed by fire in 392BC.

The honey-coloured, limestone Doric columns appear almost to grow from the dust, allowing them to blend in with this solemn place of contemplation. The columns that stand here now are mostly the result of restoration work originally done during the Italian occupation in the first half of the 20th Century.

That the Italians were often more concerned about making the grand gesture rather than strict authenticity has led to criticism of them by modern archaeologists, and the scaffolding, which is frequently a feature of the acropolis, alludes to a more thorough and wholesale restoration under the aegis of the Greek Ministry of Culture, which is a perpetual work in progress.

The original excavation of the site was carried out by Danish archaeologists under the direction of Christian Blinkenberg and Karl Frederik Kinch between 1900 and the beginning of the First World War. Looking over the southern precipice of the promontory, gazing down at the cobalt blue waters of St Paul's Bay, I couldn't help thinking that for those archaeologists from the Carlsberg Institute, going to work on a Monday morning could not have been too daunting. This natural shallow harbour has the smallest of entrances in its north-east corner making it an ideal anchorage and, legend has it, one which was taken advantage of by St Paul when he landed here to fulfil his mission to preach Christianity to the islanders. Turning around looking north across the Grand Harbour you can see for miles along the coast in the direction of Rhodes Town.

Back in the lower town I headed out from the centre wherever my weary legs would take me. This happened to be an unassuming courtyard restaurant just opening for lunch which served me bakaliaros skordalia. These small chunks of salted cod are soaked in water then dried, floured and seasoned with pepper before frying in olive oil until golden and then doused in a thick sauce made of pureed potatoes, olive oil, almond and copious bulbs of crushed garlic. I followed this with an avgolemono soup, dipping the chunks of bread from the basket in a bowl of zesty lemon chicken broth taking the salty edge off the ice cold Amstel I had ordered.

Wandering down the path to an almost deserted St Paul's Bay we found a shady spot to siesta away an afternoon in the shadow of the acropolis before an early evening swim as the lights illuminating the columns and ramparts above against a star-studded sky signalled time for dinner on a rooftop terrace.

Don't Panic!

The first time I visited Rhodes, I flew to Athens' then airport, Ellinikon International, before swapping terminals to catch the domestic service to the island. The connecting flight was an evening one and we did the short transfer to the west terminal, checked in our luggage and boarded the plane. Although my Greek was not too bad, the hurriedly delivered message over the PA system as we prepared to taxi to the runway passed me by.

Suddenly we were surrounded by fellow passengers shouting and screaming, and cabin crew wrestling to reopen the aircraft doors. The only people still sitting in our seats, I enquired what was happening. Amid the panic, we were somewhat alarmed to be told there was a bomb on board!

Even before the aircraft steps had been attached to the fuselage flight attendants, who had prematurely released the doors, had to restrain passengers from leaping onto the runway. With some order restored we filed off the plane and back into the departure lounge. There we began the long wait for the situation to be resolved. A passenger, who claimed to do the trip regularly, assured us that this was a regular occurrence and that we would not be going anywhere that night. With which he took himself off to find a hotel.

With nowhere else to go we waited with the other passengers, until we were told to reclaim our baggage that had been unloaded onto the runway. Standing over the pile of cases on the tarmac were four armed guards. Claiming our luggage we dragged it back to the terminal and, after what seemed like hours, were asked to check it in again. Sitting on the runway was one solitary bag. Uniformed men were surrounding it with sandbags.

Back on the plane we prepared for take off and taxied to the end of the runway. The engines suddenly increased their volume, ready to catapult the aircraft skywards. Suddenly they were throttled back and the pilot appeared from the cockpit and walked through the plane.

I asked the passing stewardess what was wrong, '*tipota*' she replied with a shrug, 'nothing'. Then she explained the pilot needed to use the toilet prior to take off. Fortunately we are not nervous fliers, but that experience certainly put our constitutions to the test. I sometimes wonder if the passenger who had checked himself into a hotel found himself with no luggage the next morning.

Old Kamiros – A City from a Golden Age

Lulled by the bay of Lindos, staying would have been easy. An early morning walk to the ancient Temple of Athena, followed by a languid lunch at anchor in the cockpit of our little sloop had taken their toll. The columns atop the acropolis now floated in the burnished mid-afternoon sky as we awoke from siesta, staring up from the warm pine planking of the deck. Our state was of such somnolence that, like Homer's Lotus Eaters, we were loath to leave. But Odysseus-like, our skipper was a hard task-master and a quick dip shook out the last vestiges of siesta.

While at anchor we hoisted the main bringing our bow into the gentlest zephyr. As the grapnel broke the surface, we unfurled the foresail spinning the bow out of the wind until balanced by the sheeted main we headed out hard by the peninsular we had scaled just hours earlier. The tiny entrance to the bay named after St Paul slipped past to starboard in the blink of an eye. The apostle is said to have visited here *en route* to Patara, in what is now Turkey, on his third Missionary journey.

As our boat bends to the wind its timber creaking, she settles into a southerly course. Our plan is to sail through the night to make the 70-odd nautical mile passage to Kamiros, another of the ancient triumvirate of Rhodian cities, and make landfall by morning. The wind had filled in during the afternoon and settled into a comfortable Force 3 caressing the water just enough to provide the occasional ruffle of spray as we slapped seawards on a long starboard tack.

The sails cleated, the slightest of tweaks to the tiller kept a comfortable list to leeward as we settled to enjoy the last few hours before sunset. I had been to Lindos on several occasions, but had not visited Kamiros before, the nearest I had got was the excellent Art Deco fish taverna on the beach below where the ancient city lies. I make no apologies for this as the food and welcome at this bustling restaurant on one of the few sandy strips of shoreline on the west coast is enough to divert anyone's attention. Whole char-grilled sea bream, seasoned with crystalline sea salt, doused in lemon, garlic and olive oil sauce is a memory I will have to put aside if we are to achieve our aim this time.

Our hope was to circumnavigate half the island, turning north again around the Cape of Prasonissi, skirting the west coast past Cape Armenistis. Here the waist of the island narrows as if tightly belted as we set the last lay line for our destination. Unlike Lindos the burghers of Kamiros were not seafaring men, making their living off the land away from the coast. As such there is no suitable harbour and we had to pray that the weather would hold, as it was our intention to anchor off and make the shore in our inflatable tender.

The signs were good and the May weather more stable than it can be in the parched months of midsummer where the ebb and flow of the barometer can whisk up precocious winds at the drop of a hat. As the sun made its descent behind Rhodes to our west, a sliver of moon shared the half light until the orange globe was snuffed out beyond the island coast and a riot of stars came out to play in the night sky.

We stow the main and crank the reluctant engine to life as the wind follows the sun into hiding. As a chill takes to the air, we reach for our thermal tops. With no need to rely on the gimbals to find the equilibrium for a brew, we spark the stove under a *kafebriko* of sugar and Greek coffee and serve up four small cups, *metrio*, to take the edge off the cold, before toasting the night in ouzo as we forge forward alone, our wake leaving the only scar across the star-strewn panoply.

We decide to take two, four-hour watches, starting at 9 o'clock. I still don't turn in until 10, reluctant to let this evening go. Bleary eyed at 1.00am emerging from the forepeak to take the helm, the low thudding of the engine breaking the very stillness of the night which made its use necessary. A kaleidoscope of stars shines out of a universe of sky and sea that wrapped itself around our world. This is a night where nothing breaks that glorious monotony of the invisible black horizon where sea meets sky. My watch goes by in the twinkling of a shooting star and it is time to go below to catch some sleep before morning.

Only one hour into my slumber and a shaft of light breaks through the porthole, coaxing us awake. We arise to join the others on deck and are welcomed with yoghurt, nuts and honey, almond pie and freshly-squeezed sweetened lemon juice with ice.

The sun is rising from the heart of the Knight's Castle of Monolithos high upon its promontory to our east, like a ball fused with white heat fired from some glorious celestial cannon. From the sea the fortress looks even more imposing than it does from on shore. The stubs of the broken teeth of its battlements viewed from here do not detract from my imaginings of its heyday when the black standard bearing the Maltese cross fluttered from its ramparts. I daydream about the erstwhile Knights of St John who became the Knights Hospitaller and have a sudden realisation that their pennant is that which is now used by St John Ambulance back at home. This had not occurred to me before, but both the name and the healing connection surely could not be coincidence. A little research confirms that the modern day organization does indeed have roots in the Hospitaller Order of Jerusalem, Rhodes and Malta.

As we cross Kerameni Bay the castle towers some 800 feet above us perched on the enormous crag of Monopetra, which means 'single rock'. We are in the shadow of a stronghold that has stood here since 1476 AD when the Knights felt the need to reinforce the outposts of their island empire by building on top of defenses already installed high on the hillside in Byzantine times. As we sail north this bastion is reluctant to let us go, and holds its diminishing realm in grasp for some time as we skirt the densely pined forest on this hilly coastline.

As the sun begins to impose itself, enough breeze rises for us to break out the sails and coast along on a comfortable reach across a gently rolling sea, little troubled by the fledgling wind. Rounding Cape Armenistis, Monolithos is at last shaken from view and in the distance, off our port bow, we can see the islands of Chalki, Alimnia and their acolytes. Once a centre for sponge fishing, Chalki's three hundred or so inhabitants now rely on income from tourists seeking a secluded break to eek out a living, and boat trips there can be found from Rhodes Town and less regularly on various craft departing the west coast. Further away still I believe I can see the outline of Symi, shimmering on the horizon, but this may just be a mirage as it is some miles off. Thankfully the sea retains its benevolent state as we approach our destination. We will anchor some 50 yards offshore and make landfall by dinghy, leaving our skipper onboard in case the wind should rise or our anchor drag.

As soon as we reach shore and drag the inflatable up the beach we are heralded by the friendly hawkeyed waiter from the taverna, and resist the temptation to accept his invitation of some refreshment before we begin our ascent. Promising to take him up on his offer upon our return, we head inland and upwards.

From the coast the ancient site of Kamiros is only around half a mile uphill. It being the middle of the day the hot air laced with pine resin dries the throat as we catch our breath. I am surprised how quiet the site is as we approach, for it is situated in the most beautiful of spots and is magnificent in the extent of its completeness. On the way our conversation is of how much of Rhodes addictive charm lies in its compactness, in how much variety of architecture and landscape is crammed into this accessible island, which could comfortably be driven around in a day. The white, dust brown and reds of the settlement seem to echo these thoughts, its self-containment giving a sense of completeness in the mind's eye, which belies the fact that the city was abandoned more than two millennia ago. The ancient city has been described as the Greek Pompeii, but the comparison does not bear scrutiny.

It would seem that the relinquished town was not destroyed by natural disaster. Although it had fallen victim to earthquakes in 226 BC and 142 BC, it was the natural gravitational pull of Rhodes City itself, the town that Kamiros had been instrumental in founding in 408 BC, which was ultimately responsible for its demise.

It is clear as we pass through the entrance into what was the commercial district that this town was not built by a warring tribe. The defences are so in absence, that rumours of its people being subject to pirate attack which may have hastened their fleeing to the safety of the new capital may be true. But it is here that the first significant settlement on the island is thought to have been built. The Dorians can lay claim to this, but lower down the slopes towards the sea is evidence that the Mycenaeans had first inhabited the area centuries earlier.

Indeed it was the discovery of an ancient grave amongst the reforested area of hillside running down to the sea, which led to the uncovering of an Achaean necropolis near the village of Kalovarda. This alerted archaeologists to the site's possibilities in the mid 19th Century. But it was the Italians who must be credited with much of the excavation work that we can see today, bringing an archaeological rigour, which defined the boundaries of the site before their systematic revealing of its entirety. That it was abandoned and ultimately forgotten until then is probably the reason that the city still retains so much of its integrity. It has a conformity to its origins that has not been sullied by layers of generational building.

Looking across the three-tiered site, I get the sense that there are few places that are so in tune with their environment. A small lizard scurries across the fountain square as I look south up the levels of this man-made amphitheatre cut into the hillside. The columns of the Temple of Athena Kamiros rise up from the apogee, dominating the lower levels of the settlement.

Against a backdrop of pine trees growing from the sparse, white rock the Doric columns watch over an army of cicadas sounding out their perpetual paradiddle. I am in the heart of the community space of the town, where people would congregate in the partly-shaded areas to pass the time and argue politics. In those days the square would have been graced with statues to the gods and goddesses, now long gone, only their inscribed marble plinths remaining.

Back down the hill is an area of stone altars laid out in ranks. Each bearing the inscription to a god to whom an appropriate, sometimes grizzly, sacrifice might be made. The largest is to the sun god Helios. Others to lesser deities show the polytheistic nature of the original inhabitants, with tabernacles to the likes of Hestia, the goddess of Home and

Agathos Daimon the God of Good Luck also in evidence. From the agora or market area of the town, with its small temple to Apollo abutting the fountain square, the central thoroughfare rises up through the houses of the citizens towards the acropolis.

A warren of alleyways, some barely wide enough to accommodate a laden mule, form a filigree of dusty paths to the east of the city where potters used to labour making pithoi to store the wine and oil on which the city based its wealth. Unlike the citizens of Lindos to the east, the wealthy burghers of Kamiros had not made their money by seafaring or piracy but by the more peaceful pursuit of living off the land. The lack of fortifications exemplifies their peaceful existence, and when they came together with Lindos and Ialyssos to form the political union which saw the pragmatic creation of the new city of Rhodes, it is clear that they had much to gain from having access to its seaports through which they could open up new markets for their goods. The tiny harbour of Mylantia directly below was too small, and carried too shallow a draught for any ship of significance. It is more likely that, prior to the creation of Rhodes Town under their patronage, they hauled their wares by hoof the eight or so miles to the south, and the small but deeper water jetty of the port which lies in what is now the village of Kamiros Skala.

Reaching the top of the climb we sit down on the parched earth that opens out onto a plateau. Remains of walls, columns and plinths stand in memorium to a time when this was the huge colonnaded avenue of the stoa stretching across the whole summit of the acropolis itself, laid out in homage to the crowning temple of Athena Kamiros which stood behind. This is where the merchants would do their trading out of shop fronts and their deals in offices with the local farmers, securing their finest produce to hawk to citizens in the hinterland.

A giant cistern dating from the 6th Century BC lies to our right, with steps leading down into its bowels. This is one of two such storage reservoirs that supplied the city with water, the other being just off the Fountain Square below. Lawrence Durrell had talked of hearing the gurgling of water running below when he visited in 1947 and even went underground to explore the water conduits with Paddy Leigh Fermor and Xan Fielding, but I can hear nothing. We have to open our plastic bottles to secure a drink, and quench our thirst with mineral water.

Using these moments to take stock, it is hard to imagine a more perfect place to live and do business, what is left of the crowning temple gives a clue, but does not do justice, to what it looked like. Shaken to its foundations by the earthquake of 226 BC, what we see now is the remains of walls from the temple that replaced the Doric incarnation of the house of worship, which had collapsed. But as you look back down over the stoa, northwards over the ancient city and west across the sea below, it is hard for your imagination not to come to the rescue and fill in the architectural gaps which nature has rubbed out of the picture. If ever there might have been a golden age of Hellenistic Greece, the remains of this wonderful town and the images it conjures up epitomize it. Why its inhabitants ever deserted such a spot remains a mystery. But thank whatever gods those citizens may have worshipped that they did, otherwise we would not have this boundless treasure left to us.

A welcome sea breeze is starting to come in off the sea, filling in where the hot air ascends off the parched ground. Back at sea level, we return in the dinghy to collect our skipper who is sure enough of the anchor now to risk coming ashore for some food at the beachside Taverna Old Kamiros. Needing something to pick us up after the night sail and climb, we order a shared plate bursting with golden kalamari, deep red king prawns, mussels glistening in a wine and butter emulsion and shiny-eyed bream adorned with wedges of lemon and bejeweled with large crystals of sea salt. Bread, salad and a harsh wine chilled to just off freezing to knock the edge off it completed the leisurely feast which we ate staring out at our sloop drifting, her head following the shifting wind, riding to anchor in the bay.

Celebrations of Life

In Greece Easter is a much bigger celebration than Christmas and name days are far bigger than birthdays. Before I understood the concept of the name day I was amazed at why so many pupils arrived at the school where I taught in a state of high excitement all apparently celebrating their birthday on the same day.

I expressed my surprise to my boss Manolis who explained that most Greek children are named after saints, martyrs or legendary figures. Consequently, throughout their lives, they celebrate their name days alongside other people similarly named. So if christened Giorgos or Giorgia, on St George's Day they celebrate with a host of other people who share the same name.

Easter is the most important single festival in Greece and is a time for much solemn contemplation preceding some serious feasting and drinking. In spring, the weather is warm and the countryside full of promise, lush and bathed in colour. It is a perfect time that is wholly appropriate for the celebration of the resurrection of Christ.

Many Greek Orthodox Christians still fast throughout Lent, eating no meat or animal products. By Holy Thursday the sense of expectation of the coming celebrations is tangible, and families prepare by dying eggs red as a symbol of life, ready for them to be eaten on Easter Day. In the evening of that same day, women go to church and decorate a casket with flowers ready to receive the icon of Christ on Good Friday.

The following day is one of mourning the crucifixion of Christ. The priest will take down the icon of our Lord from the cross in the church and wrap it in linen before placing it in a casket that is symbolic of the tomb in which Jesus was buried. In the evening the casket is carried at the head of a procession around the town or village to the accompaniment of hymns.

After the procession, people retire to a local taverna where they eat a dinner of seafood but still no meat. Shellfish, squid, taramasalata and salads bring welcome respite to those who have been fasting.

By the evening of the following day the churches are packed for the service of the resurrection, which begins an hour before midnight. In villages with small churches, the people spill outside where the service is relayed to them through loudspeakers. During the service the lights are turned out and the congregation light candles they have brought with them from the Holy Light passed round by the Priest. Just before midnight the Priest leads his flock outside the church and as the hour strikes he chants *'Christos anesti' (*Christ is risen).

The announcement is the cue for fireworks to be set off and in some places guns are shot in the air, families and friends wish each other well before heading home. Keeping your candle alight is supposed to be a sign of good luck for the coming year and making a sign of the cross above a doorway with the soot from the flame is said to protect the family who live there.

With that the fast is over. Traditionally families will eat a soup made from the organs of the lamb they will roast for the following day's feast. The dyed eggs are then cracked against those of others and the person whose shell smashes last will have more good luck!

Easter Day itself is one of massive celebration, a lamb or a goat is roasted, often on a spit and a massive outdoor party ensues with music, drinking and dancing well into the night.

Fish for Lunch

Young George cast off the stern line from the outer harbour wall at Kolimbia where *Maria* was moored and scuttled for'ard to man the winch that Captain Lefteris set in motion from the cockpit. Whether ironic or a nickname from many years ago which had stuck, Young George, although probably nearing 70 years of age, was certainly very sprightly. No sooner had he stowed the anchor and the gangplank than he set about baiting hooks on the trolling lines with shrimps. Clear of our mooring, Lefteris gave the twin outdrives their head as they thrust us southwards, traversing the long beach of the bay. Sunshades were up as enthusiastic sun worshippers made an early start with their devotions. It was apparent that Helios would not disappoint today as not a cloud showed its face as we settled in to our passage on a sea as smooth as baize.

Lefteris throttled back and the boat dropped down off her plane to allow Young George to let out the lines astern, one to port and one to starboard, one armed with spinners the other baited hooks. He then turned his attention to the rods, which stood in holders on the guardrails, adjusting the ledgers and baiting the hooks before returning them to their sheaths.

At the end of the long bay the shoreline grew more rocky and indented with tiny inlets like secret bathing spots for sea nymphs. With the echo sounder bleeping and Captain Lefteris focused on his sonar fish finder screen, the weather couldn't have been more perfect for me, but Lefteris muttered something about it being too hot and sunny for the fish. Not to be deterred Young George heaved the anchor overboard before lowering some plastic buckets over the side to fill them in anticipation of our forthcoming catch. Lefteris told us that if we got a bite we must shout 'fish' so George could come and disgorge our prey in case it was too dangerous to handle, like a *skorpidi* or scorpion fish. Their sting can be extremely painful and if stung it is advisable to seek medical attention, although locals will tell you vinegar will ease the symptoms. These pests along with the equally toxic grey weaver fish that inhabit the sandy bottom of the seabed are both to be avoided. Both species can frequently be seen when snorkelling and, if disturbed, will quickly swim away. The danger is in the unlikely event of stepping on one or, if fishing, taking your catch off the hook. Scorpidi can also be seen on the menu in many a restaurant and once devoid of their poisonous spikes are delicious either grilled or in a fish stew!

The otherwise benign waters that surround Rhodes hold little to fear, although there are a few nasties that are worth mentioning here to the unwary traveller.

Top of the list are jellyfish that can drift inshore and lurk, barely visible, just beneath the surface in readiness for the unsuspecting swimmer. I have been stung on three occasions and it is not pleasant. I have not tried it, but urine is said to take away the sting, although vinegar is as effective and antihistamine tablets or a cream can also ease the inflammation.

Black spiky sea urchins also linger, clinging to underwater rocks. Stepping on them can prove agonizing, although unlikely to do lasting damage apart from that to your pride from the subsequent – and inevitable – embarrassing hop up the beach.

Removing the broken-off spikes with tweezers is the uncomfortable solution to this one. If you want to get your own back, there are some tavernas that serve up the roe of the little blighters with olive oil and lemon juice as a mezze. For those who adhere to the adage that revenge is best served cold, believe me – in this instance – this is not the case. To be fair, there are many Greeks who would disagree with my culinary assessment of this all-too-plentiful ingredient.

The trolling lines were reeled back aboard, and George set to rebaiting the barren hooks. I could feel almost imperceptible bites on my hook but every time I struck, the line returned empty. Judging by the number of times I had to replace the shrimps on my hook, something had been nibbling. After twenty or so minutes, none of the rods had caught anything, so losing patience Lefteris decided to try elsewhere.

We secured our hooks on the bail bars of our reels and holstered our rods and set off further south. To starboard a sweeping bay opened up, and even from out at sea I could detect the extent of its perfection. Flat and stretching way inland, the burnished sand only interrupted by the occasional shade-giving rock around the periphery it appeared to only bear the beach paraphernalia so essential to modern tourism at its northern end. The rest of the beach was deserted. Young George told me this was Tsambika and I noted it down, with the intention of returning. I would have liked to have beached the tender there and then and taken the path up the mighty cone-shaped hill that overlooks the bay. George assured me that the effort to climb the 307 steps, which complete the path to a tiny monastery, was worth it, not least for the magnificent view. He also related a confused anecdote about an icon, which was too much for my limited language skills to comprehend. I looked the story up later and discovered that the chapel was erected on the site of a miracle. It sits nearly 1000 feet in the air looking down on the bay we had been crossing, and houses a particularly splendid icon of the annunciation which, rumour has it, was miraculously transported here from its original home in Cyprus.

The legend goes that some centuries ago, what is now known as the icon of Panagia Tsambika used to reside in a monastery some 240 miles to the south east on Cyprus. One night a shepherd, out with his flock on the hillside the other side of the valley, noticed a light shining from the mountain. Ignoring this phenomenon for two nights, on the third his curiosity got the better of him and he decided to investigate.

Frightened of the unknown, he corralled a group of villagers who strapped on their arms and followed him up the mountain towards the source of the mystery. Following the light they emerged at the summit, to find a lone cypress tree, in its branches rested an illuminated icon of the Virgin Mary. Incredulous, the shepherd and his entourage removed the icon from the tree and returned with it to the village, but the icon was not to be denied its favoured spot at the summit of the mountain and mysteriously made its own way back to the tree. Three times this happened before the villagers succumbed to the wishes of the Panagia, and built a chapel to house the icon. The mountain on which she now resides is named after the word *tsamba*, which meant 'spark' in the local Rhodian dialect.

The Cypriots were not best pleased that their icon had been relocated, and they tracked it down and tried to remove it three times, smuggling it back to its native shores. They even burned the back of the icon to identify it, but each time the painting returned to where it hangs today, the charred markings clear for all to see.

The miraculous homing instinct of the insistent icon is not its only mystical quality. During the period of Ottoman rule, the wife of a local Turkish Pasha found herself unable to conceive. Putting her faith in the miraculous icon she prayed to the Virgin and did penance by eating the wick from the vigil light, which burned by its side. She duly became pregnant, although her husband was loathe to accept the intervention of the icon. That was until the baby was born, when the child emerged into the world holding the wick from the lamp that his mother had swallowed. Since then the monastery has had the reputation of helping women to get pregnant, and on its feast day in September they often climb the steps to the monastery barefoot or even on their knees, in obeisance to the Panagia and to ask for her to favour them. Only in Rhodes will you hear the name Tsampika for a girl or Tsambikos for a boy, the children named after the beneficence of the miraculous icon that undoubtedly feels this to be the place she truly belongs.

Lefteris still had the bit between his teeth and was determined to track down the illusive fish, as though failure would somehow have reflected on his manhood. We ploughed our furrow of wash southward further across the bay, passing a small beach with tiny open boats moored just offshore lying beneath a village further up the limestone cliffs. Consulting the chart, I identified this as Stegna.

As we left the tiny resort astern Young George leaped into action as though some unseen instinct had alerted him to some fish taking interest in his trolling lines. He reeled in, and sure enough the hooks were alive with a modest, lustrous catch of chub mackerel and what looked like small bream among others, maybe mullet or wrasse. Lefteris was all smiles and headed for a small bay in which we anchored and cast out our rods. This time the success from the trolls was repeated and we felt bites on our lines almost every time we raised the bait from the seabed.

Soon the buckets were brimming with a myriad of fish and we were ready for a cooling swim. As we dived off the stern of the boat, the crew set up a simple barbeque on the beach. The dispatched fish where gutted and had their skin slashed with a knife before being dusted in seasoned flour and dropped into a pan of hot oil. In another pan rough chopped garlic and rosemary were cooked in some butter before red wine and red wine vinegar were added and the whole sauce reduced.

The fish and the sauce were served with bread and salad with salty feta in lustrous green olive oil. The dish is a makeshift version of Psari Savoro, which can be found in any number of restaurants throughout Greece, the fish made to use it as variable as the exact nature and proportions of the recipe. As an experience, this serving was the best I have tasted.

We were to return to Tsambika sooner than anticipated but, I have to admit, not at first to visit the icon of the Virgin. That same day travelling back from Kolimbia to Lindos along the coast road we felt in need of some refreshment, particularly in the form of ice cream. Just past the turn off for Tsambika beach we turned off at a sign advertising the Panorama Taverna. What a find! We would not usually have stopped at a restaurant beside a main road but, set back from the traffic, this hidden enclave with its tables laid out beneath a pergola entwined with a mature vine, is the perfect spot to sit and enjoy whatever takes your fancy.

Overlooking the rocky hillside that slips away to Tsambika beach, with the sea we had so recently been fishing in the distance, we indulged our whim with a wonderful bowl full of ice cream and fresh fruit. Since then we have returned many times to dine there and have never been disappointed. In the evenings as the sun goes down, under the twinkling lights nestling in the vines above, with the smells of the herbs used to brush the delicious fish and meat cooked over the coals on the outside barbecue, here is a secret most tourists do not know about but many Greeks do, as it is frequently full.

The Language Barrier

Daunting, that is how most people confronted with learning Greek find it. In conversation, Greeks speak so fast it is hard to identify individual words. As for writing… You have to learn a completely new alphabet and loads of sounds that don't even exist in other languages.

To add to these seemingly insurmountable stumbling blocks, there are distinct differences in regional accents. And just to top this off, most Greeks can – and like to – speak English, so practicing is nigh on impossible!

Don't be put off. Start with a few words. These can go a long way, and any attempt by a foreigner to speak the language will always be complimented. Learn a few basic words and then try to learn some phrases.

In the beginning, not being able to read the language can be a positive thing, as it forces you to rely on your ears. I found that by looking at words as pictures helped. Then trying to match these pictures to word sounds subsequently got me more familiar with their constituent letter sounds. Subsequently, I slowly began to read at a basic level.

I started to learn a phrase a day and with the encouragement of my Greek friends who would correct me if I went wrong became, if not exactly fluent, at least able to get by in day-to-day situations. Greek people are amazed and flattered at any attempt made to speak a few words in their own language and are happy to show off their superior mastery of English if you get stuck.

The Greeks are particularly sympathetic about language issues. As recently as 1976, there were two forms of Greek in use. The first was the official, state-sanctioned language, *katharevousa*, which largely had been invented at the time modern Greece was being created in the 19th Century. The other, the everyday tongue spoken by the majority of people was known as *dhimotiki*, or demotic Greek.

The advocates of *katharevousa* saw it as a purer version of the language with its roots in the classical Greek of the Hellenic period; on the other hand *dhimotiki* had developed organically through the everyday spoken word of the people and could legitimately claim to be a more authentic descendant of ancient Greek.

Lawyers, government, the church and all arms of officialdom, used *katharevousa* and it was also the language used in educational institutions. It excluded a great many people. *Katharevousa* was in effect elitist, its users considering *dhimotiki*, and the people who spoke it, to be vulgar. Speakers of the common tongue saw *katharevousa* as a weapon of conservative, linguistic purists who used language as a way to preserve their status and control over the people.

Many intellectuals championed the cause of *dhimotiki*, among them was the author Nikos Kazantzakis who wrote in it. But the most influential reason for the demise of *katharevousa* was education. How was the state to educate the mass of its population in a language they not only didn't understand, but were resistant to learning?

If Greece was going to become a modern, developed nation, it could not afford to sideline the majority of its population from access to educational opportunities. *Konstantinos* Karamanlis, the first Prime Minister to take office after the fall of the military dictatorship in 1974, sanctioned *dhimotiki* as the official language of the country two years later. In passing its adoption into law the use of *dhimotiki* became symbolic of the wider democratic measures brought in by Karamanlis to establish the constitution of the modern Greek republic.

Inevitably anyone who takes on the task of trying to learn the language will be confronted with problems of dialect. Even an Athenian will sometimes struggle to understand a broad island accent. But never have I felt belittled by my failure to get my words out right and have always been rewarded for my efforts by a sense of inclusion. It's well worth making the effort.

The Rhythm of Life

Out in the countryside the overwhelming sound of summer in Rhodes is that of the cicada. The clicking noise is not, as is often thought, the sound of them rubbing their wings or legs together, but the result of the male insects vibrating membranes in their abdomens which act like tiny echo chambers creating the distinctive sound.

The buzzing is a mating song used to attract females and is competitive in nature. When one male starts his call all the others in the surrounding area quickly join him until the noise reaches a crescendo. The name cicada is Latin, and literally means 'buzzer'. The Greek word for them is the more onomatopoeic *tzitzikas*.

Although the rasping of cicadas is commonplace, strangely absent is the sound of birdsong. Wild birds, except the larger protected species, are often hunted and eaten in rural areas, leaving the numbers of songbirds in the wild considerably diminished. Strangely, it is in the towns, where people frequently keep caged birds, that you are more likely to hear birdsong. From many a balcony, resplendent with blooming flowers the sweet sound of singing birds softens the roar of the traffic below.

Lindos would appear to be an exception which proves this rule as there, in the rafters of arches which span the lanes in the old town, hundreds of swallows roost and manage to provide the weary traveler with a potent dawn chorus on days when the church bells have not already risen them from their slumbers.

Anthony Quinn Bay

The sunset in Rhodes is like no other I have seen. From a burst of fiery orange it starts to sink behind the hills over the town turning them from brown to black. The medieval fortress and Turkish minarets hang on as best they can to the last minutes of light reflecting yellow, green then blue before becoming shadows silhouetted against a sky rapidly losing definition.

The strong afternoon sea breeze had dropped away to a mere whisper as we coasted out of Mandraki, the moon adequately supplementing our navigation lights. The gentle ripple of the wash of tiny caiques leaving harbour for a night's fishing barely made any impression on our equilibrium, as we swung the helm over and headed south along the coast.

Ten minutes out even the faintest of zephyrs had deserted us and we cranked *Birba's* motor until it reluctantly came to life, propelling us at a stately 5 knots along Rhodes' east coast. By the trailing log we had travelled 10 miles when, through the beam of our handheld spotlight, we found our destination and turned towards shore.

Rhodes—A Notebook

As we headed into the coastline it opened up into a bay surrounded on all sides by the dark shadows of the wooded hills. I went forward to lean off the bow with a torch and Dean on the helm kept one eye on the echo sounder as we felt our way in over the rock-strewn shallows.

We threw an anchor out astern and I dived into the still warm water and swam a bow line ashore making fast around a rock on the beach. With the engine turned off the silence was suddenly deafening. We had reached our destination of Anthony Quinn Bay.

Hard to get to by day in those days, at nighttime it was deserted. Named after the Mexican-American so beloved of Greeks for his portrayal of Alexis Zorba in the 1964 Michael Cacoyannis directed film of *Zorba the Greek*, the actor bought the land surrounding the bay after falling in love with the spot when he was filming the *Guns of Navarone* here. It was Anthony Quinn who was responsible for driving a road through to the bay. Before he purchased the land it was only accessible by sea or rough mountain tracks.

That he fell in love with it is hardly surprising. Sitting on the coachroof of Dean and Jo's boat in overwhelming silence with the stars giving a perfect show against a sky unpolluted by any other surrounding light it is difficult not to reflect on our place in the scheme of things.

Even though Quinn died in 2001 there is still controversy surrounding the ownership of the land which was seized back by the Greek government in the 1990s despite being sold to the actor for a nominal sum in recognition of his work in promoting tourism on the island and opening an international centre for artists and filmmakers there. The dispute is still continuing, with none other than US Secretary of State Hilary Clinton taking up the cause on her visits to Greece for bilateral talks in 2011.

For us back in 1986 we new nothing of this but spent one of the most spellbinding nights on deck under the stars. As dawn broke the hidden cove revealed another side of its glory. The rising sun shone straight into the bay, some of its early rays bouncing off the surface of the water while others pierced down illuminating the submerged rocks below. Surrounding the beach, pine trees run in places down the hillsides right to the sea, their roots bathed by the lapping water.

We breakfasted on fresh peaches, yoghurt, walnuts and honey before casting off, weighing anchor and setting sail for home with a gently rising south easterly breeze chivvying us along from over the starboard quarter.

I have returned to the bay several times since that magical evening, the new road making access there all too easy. It retains its beauty like an aging film star might cling to her looks, yet the work done has to an extent obscured the natural beauty that lies beneath. Although it no longer remains secluded it is still well worth a visit, particularly for the snorkelling.

Making Modern Greece

Travelling from island to island, the many differences in culture, temperament, accent and climate are evident. Despite these differences, it is clear that the similarities that bind this nation together are far stronger than any disparate elements.

The historical legacies of each region and island which constitute modern Greece are equally varied. If we take as an example the enchanted triangle of Corfu, Crete and Rhodes, their individual paths to unity only conform in that they are all widely different.

Corfu, along with the other Ionian islands, was ceded to the Kingdom of Greece in 1864 by the British; meanwhile Crete did not become part of the country until 1913; and, lagging behind, was Rhodes and the Dodecanese which were handed over by the Italians as late as 1947 following their defeat in the Second World War.

The beginnings of modern Greece as we now know it can be traced back to 1832 when, following a successful uprising against the Ottoman Turks that lasted between 1821 and 1828, the British, French and Russian governments recognized the legitimacy of the Greek state. The Treaty of London ratified this in 1932, making Greece an independent monarchy.

This new emerging country then consisted of Central Greece, the Peleponese, the Sporades and the Cyclades. But it took 115 years for this fledgling state to establish the borders as they are now. Some might see it as incredible that there was, and still is, such a force for unity; especially now in an age where many nation states are disintegrating. What was it that held the Greeks together for so long without a recognized geographical homeland? The three most important factors in that cohesion are ancient history, religion and language.

The great civilization of Classical Greece between 505 BC to the death of Alexander the Great was followed by the Hellenistic period that lasted until the Greek heartlands were conquered by the Romans in the second century BC with Rhodes formally becoming part of the empire in 164 BC. As the power of the Roman Empire in western Europe waned, it was followed by a strongly Greek-influenced Eastern Empire centered on Constantinople. This Greek speaking Byzantine Empire lasted until the Ottoman Turks overran it in 1453 AD.

Corfu placed itself under the sovereignty of Venice in 1401 AD, which was a major factor in it being the only part of the Greek-speaking Christian world to never be conquered by the Turks. Crete was not so lucky, a Venetian colony for 400 years it was finally overrun by the invaders in 1669 AD.

Likewise Rhodes, which following the fall of the Byzantine Empire had been occupied by the chivalric order of the Knights Hospitaller, finally succumbed after falling to the vast forces of Suleiman the Magnificent in 1522 AD.

Whether colonized for their own protection or conquered by an aggressive force, the Greeks as a race continued to speak their own language and worship in the Greek Orthodox faith. They also proudly held on to the knowledge that they were the living ancestors of the Ancient Greeks and that their rightful homeland was the 'cradle of civilization'.

Despite this powerful pull towards unity, it seemed that differences over politics, the constitution and even language could tear the newly-reunited nation apart. If there had not been an overriding hatred of the Ottoman Empire and an ambition to achieve the *megali idea* (great idea) of reuniting all Greek lands to their Byzantine boundaries, modern Greece might still remain nothing but a dream.

Two crucial arguments raged within the new Greece. Firstly, the fundamental political and constitutional differences between the monarchist right-wing nationalists, and the republican, liberal left who saw Greece's part in a wider European and world context. This became known as the national schism. Secondly, there was the language question.

Most Greeks spoke an everyday form of the language called *dhimotiki*, which had developed naturally through everyday usage over the centuries. Many of those in the educated elite perceived this language as a peasant tongue. They believed that if the glories of Ancient Greece were to be restored, then what was effectively a pastiche of Classical Greek should be spoken. This completely different language was known as *katharevousa* and was adopted in official documents and newspapers. This was divisive, in that few of the uneducated masses could understand it.

Monarchs came and went, military coups overthrew kings and governments alike and ultimately this inner turmoil put paid to the dream of the *megali idea*. Greece's internal struggles were responsible for it losing territory it had gained after the First World War following defeat by Kemal Ataturk's forces in 1922. This led to the great population exchange in 1923 where 1.5million Christians and 500,000 Muslims were uprooted and moved to land within the redrawn borders of Greece and Turkey.

I think it is fair to say that the country only put to rest the two issues of the national schism and the language question following the declaration of the current republic in 1974. Two years later *dhimotiki* was finally declared the official national language.

With the question of the country adopting a constitutional monarchy or being taken over by military rulers now unlikely, the political high ground of modern Greece is largely contested between the right-wing New Democracy Party and the left-wing Pan Hellenic Socialist Movement (PASOK) who have operated a revolving door policy in Government ever since.

Recently the power of the two ruling dynasties has been weakened by the economic crisis, which has seen a succession of coalition governments trying to secure the bailouts required to keep the Greek economy afloat. But there lurks an even more potent threat that has arisen out of the privations of austerity. The extreme right wing party Golden Dawn is gaining a foothold in parliament and is the antithesis of all that is good about Greece. The current recession is playing into the arms of these fascist thugs and the measures that Prime Minister Antonis Samaras has been forced to impose on his people that has caused them to suffer immense hardship has fuelled the polarization of political attitudes. Many fear that Greece is teetering on the brink of another civil war and the rise of the extreme right must fill those who remember the days of the fascist dictatorship of the colonels with dread.

Petaloudes – The Valley of the Butterflies

I was in some doubt as to whether or not to write about Petaloudes, better known as the Valley of the Butterflies. But as details about it are hard to escape on Rhodes it would be obtuse of me not to include this appealing, fertile ravine that would be unextraordinary, were it not for the butterflies that reside there. My reluctance is born of the fact that the population of butterflies that give this haven its name has in recent years been in decline.

Some 15 miles to the south west of Rhodes Town, lying in the shadow of Mount Psinthos is this unique refuge. Strictly speaking, the millions of 'butterflies' that migrate here for the summer months are a type of tiger moth that goes by the name of *callimorpha quadripunctaria himalaiensis*. Their rather grand Latin moniker alludes to where the moth was first identified, in the contrasting environment of the Himalayas. The reference to 'four' relates to the markings on the wing of the moth, which resembles that number expressed as a Roman numeral.

When at rest, the moths look an unspectacular grey colour as they carpet the trees that line the banks of the River

Pelecanos, which burbles its way through falls and pools. However, when disturbed they arise like a huge iridescent magic carpet of yellow and black with a glimpse of red as they ghost overhead. Herein lies the danger for the moths, as they retain minimal body fat, which they require just to survive. Repeated attempts by some visitors to see them fly, scaring them by clapping and shouting, has caused the premature death of thousands of moths. Fortunately warning signs appear to be improving matters and the decline has been halted in what is, after all, a protected nature park.

The small but insistent river provides a perfect microclimate for both moths and humans. The latter are attracted to this little piece of paradise by the spectacle of the moths themselves; the former by the cool and humid air exuded as the river splashes from fall to pool beneath the shade of the prolific storax trees. These Oriental sweetgum exude a smell of resin that is attractive to the moths, as well as local church communities who use it for incense. Wooden bridges weave across the river and, in the early months of summer, purple blasts of colour ring out from the bell-like campanulas bravely clinging to the rocky terrain. The walk is leisurely, and it is well worth crossing the road at the top of the valley and walking on for another quarter of an hour or so to the tiny monastery of Panagia Kalopetra.

The story goes that the church was built by a Greek prince, Alexander Ypsilantis. In 1784 the Turks had usurped him from his kingdom of Vlachia, in what is now Romania. Banished to a life on Rhodes, he lived as the abbot of this foundation. Looking back it is easy to empathise with the words of celebrated local poet Theofanis Bogiannos when he writes: 'There isn't any place in Greece like this, so beautiful, so blessed with greenery, colour, such winged souls, so many human souls, and cool, singing cicadas, so much joy on peoples faces' – and the view back down the valley is one to savour.

Greece's Modern Musical Soul

In winter Greece changes faces, and its society moves indoors. Restaurants and music venues situated off the main tourist tracks throw open their doors to local trade. It is now that the *boites* open up. Dark and intimate, lit by candlelight and often below street level, they play host to the *rebetika* music of Greece.

It is hard to find an equivalent to *rebetika* in western music; although it does have the shared sentiment of much Blues. It is sad, soulful and fiercely individualistic. It encapsulates the story of Greece and the Greek spirit, and is inevitably a product of both these things.

The individualism it expresses and its evocation of freedom has made *rebetika* controversial over the years. The music has even been banned by a number of ruling administrations, which saw it as a threat to their authority. In the form it is recognized today, *rebetika* emerged in the early 1920s. It grew indirectly as a result of Greece's disastrous incursion into Asia Minor to try to seize Smyrna, and the other Greek inhabited regions of what is now western Turkey, from the Ottomans.

In 1922, after some initial success, the Greek forces were driven back out of Smyrna by the Turkish troops of Kemal Ataturk. Following brutal reprisals by the Turks on Smyrna's predominantly Greek population, it was agreed that all Christians would leave Ottoman territory for Greece and, likewise, Muslims living on Greek territory were to be displaced to Turkey. This mass migration created a huge refugee problem. Millions of people of both races and religions were exiled from the countries of their birth.

Up to 1.5 million people of Greek origin took the long trek to Greece. Some settled in Thessaloniki but most in Athens, from where many were helped to emigrate, often to America or Australia. Out of the refugee camps small bands of musicians emerged, playing songs in the style of their old homeland in Smyrna.

Rebetika is believed to have derived from the term *rebetis* that means petty criminal. This was probably how many of the indigenous Greek population viewed the refugees. But the music struck a chord, and the musicians were first hired in the clubs of Athens. As the refugees dispersed throughout Greece, the popularity of the music also spread. The songs are usually accompanied by bouzoukis, which had been used by the Greek population of Asia Minor before being brought into Greece by the musicians on the 'long walk'.

The early forms of these mandolin-like instruments had three pairs of strings, but nowadays instruments are made with four pairs, which are played with a plectrum. The music is frequently melancholic, dealing with themes such as loss, exile and fighting for freedom.

Numerous authoritarian rulers saw these songs as subversive and *rebetika* was banned by successive dictatorships. Yannis Metaxas in 1936; the occupying Germans during the Second World War; and the dictatorship of the Colonels between 1967 and 1974, all tried to suppress the music. They felt threatened by the individualism expressed and thought it evoked a refusal to be ruled by anyone.

My first introduction to *rebetika* was through the music of the popular female singer Charis Alexiou. Her album of traditional *rebetika* songs called *Ta Tsilika* was released in 1983. Prior to that her music had ridden the wave of *rebetika's* explosion in popularity following the fall of the Colonels in the Seventies.

As a young woman Charis collaborated with one of the most famous of all rebetika musicians, George Dalaras, on his definitive album *Mikra Asia* released in 1972.

The music is unlike that of the traditional dances played when people come together to celebrate weddings, name days or other social occasions. *Rebetika's* style is more introspective and personal. There are certain songs where people will get up to dance alone. Their right to personal time with the music is respected, the spell going unbroken by unwanted applause. No one else will take the floor until the dancer has finished and returned to their table in silence.

Cape Prasonissi – A Lunar Landscape

As it was my intention to travel south, away from the tourist hordes, I decided to take the opportunity to go by motorbike. I would not usually advocate motorcycling in the Greek Islands, but the sense of freedom it precipitated was hard to resist so I hope you'll indulge my hypocrisy. I had been assured that the road to Cape Prasonissi was good and, in May, before the height of the surfing season, relatively quiet. It is not strange that Rhodes Town with its many attractions commands such a gravitational pull on visitors, holding them in a triangle which has Lindos and Monolithos at its base and the capital at its apex. There was a feeling of wilful liberty about countering the tide and driving south out of Lindos along a road that flirted with both sea and land. Along here lay hidden coves and unspoilt beaches; tiny villages tucked away to the west of the road; and isolated villas, shuttered down awaiting a visit from their rich Athenian owners in August. Some houses were still awaiting completion, the stumps of reinforcing rods protruding through the flat roofs.

Over the years I have heard various reasons as to why so many buildings appear to remain unfinished. Some allege that this is to save on paying taxes that only become applicable when the building is finished. Others claim that this is not the case. The reason for the partially finished look of many houses is that the owners plan to extend them upwards at a future date as and when they can either afford to or need to. In Rhodes, when a couple get married it is customary for the parents to provide them with somewhere to live, so properties expand when the family situation requires it. If a couple have a daughter and can afford it, this will traditionally be a dowry apartment.

In these times of severe austerity, another reason may be that the land owner has just run out of the money to complete, or a contractor has gone bust.

As I approach the south of the island, the road swings inland, cutting off its most southerly tip as it heads towards the Aegean coast on the west of the island. Along this road lies the sleepy village of Katavia. It has the feel of an outpost, lying indolent on a border to nowhere, and indeed it is the most southerly village on the island. Surrounded by flat arable land, its 500 or so residents make a good living off the plain it inhabits. Some houses here have long been deserted; others show evidence of a former grandeur. The village at one time would have been home to many more people and the Knights of Rhodes turned it into a redoubt. The Hospitallers added fortifications to defend the local farmers from the tyranny of pirate bands who raided along the secluded coasts of the south, where the Aegean Sea returns to meet its mother the Mediterranean.

I stop at a cafeneon to quench my thirst. Along with my Greek coffee and water, the woman who serves me, dressed in widow's weeds, brings a small carafe of raki and a plate of *mezzes*, small fish, stuffed vine leaves, bread and olives. On leaving, my offers to pay for anything but the coffee are waved away as I take my leave to head for the cape.

The road is an extraordinary switchback ride through a unique landscape that has an almost lunar feel. I can see some way behind and beyond as I weave the five or so miles coastwards through this rock-strewn wilderness. I am totally alone save for the occasional swallow riding the low-level thermals thrown up by the shallow hills. Out of this limestone desert, the aroma of sage, thyme and rosemary confirm the existence of life and every now and then I glimpse delicate orchid-like flowers timidly peeking from behind rocks or in the sparse shade of a stunted holm oak.

Topping a small hill, Prasonissi lies below, and what a sight it is. To the west surf is rolling in, but to the east the sea is calm. Prasonissi means 'green island', and compared to the scrub-like phrygana surrounding the magnificent beach beneath me the name seems appropriate enough. At the moment Prasonissi is not really an island as it is joined to mainland Rhodes by a sandy isthmus which keeps the roaring

Aegean from the serene Mediterranean. But during the winter months, when colder weather and increased precipitation causes an increase in the water level, this rocky promontory embraces its full status as an island. Parking up near a surf shop, I set off across the narrow, sandy causeway out to the island. A track climbs south across this deserted peninsula leading at its extremity to a lone lighthouse, guiding sailors around this rugged cape.

A few windsurfers and kite-surfers have taken to the waves in the western bay, exhibiting an extraordinary mastery of the conditions. It is understandable how, in high summer, this spot is a Mecca for water sports' enthusiasts, although this has come at some price for the environment. The caretta caretta, or loggerhead turtle, has a favoured breeding ground some five miles to the north near Cape Germata and used to come south to lay its eggs in the soft sand of the beach here. A combination of the vast numbers of tourists in the summer and the compacting of the sand by vehicles being driven on the beach has, sadly, made sightings of the turtle in the area something of a rarity recently.

I return to the beach and take the opportunity for a swim in the sheltered bay, the water is still refreshingly cool, not having yet warmed up from months of summer sunshine, which by August can make it like swimming in soup. The sunsets here are supposed to be the best on the island, and I can certainly believe it, but today I cannot stay.

Hats Off for Freedom

To the uninitiated, driving in Rhodes can seem intimidating. The first time I ventured out, it was nerve wracking. Leaving the airport I grasped the wheel tightly, on the edge of my seat I asked for complete silence in the car. Wrong! This is not the way to approach the adventure of driving on Greek roads.

The only way to survive is to relax and not be panicked by other drivers. Sit back, wind down the window hang out an arm and go at whatever speed you are comfortable with. The whole experience is more like cruising along a waterway, where avoidance of oncoming vehicles or those overtaking is the only priority.

Realizing that the white lines on your right do not delineate a hard shoulder is crucial. This is more of an intermittent crawler lane that it is perfectly acceptable to drive in. It is often the only place to find some road space if the oncoming traffic is overtaking three deep or you are being hooted at from behind an impatient driver.

At the roadside all over Rhodes stand little shrines. Miniature churches which bear testament to one of the country's least enviable records. Almost without fail Greece tops the European Community chart for road deaths.

That they notch up almost three times the number of fatalities per 100,000 people per year as the UK is quite some achievement. Particularly considering the much lower volume of traffic.

To visitors' eyes, some of the driving is reckless at best and often appears downright suicidal. On roads that are littered with blind bends, unprotected sheer drops and indifferent surfaces, the relaxed attitude to any *Highway Code* accounts largely for the abundance of shrines.

This, coupled with the knowledge that on some Greek islands around a third of all drivers do not possess a valid driving license and have never taken a lesson, let alone a driving test, means the incentives for going into the shrine building business must be high! Indeed off-the-peg shrines can be bought alongside concrete barbecues in hardware stores and some garden centres.

The news is not all bad. The shrines are offerings to God not only in remembrance of those who lost their lives, but also by those thanking God that they survived. In terms of votive offerings its a win, win situation for the Good Lord. Inside the shrines are usually a bottle of holy oil, an icon, a lighted candle and sometimes a picture of the victim. These are lovingly maintained by the families of the deceased, or people giving thanks that they have survived a crash.

It is illegal to ride a motorbike, moped or scooter in Greece without a crash helmet. I suppose that slightly more people do wear them now than did in the early Eighties when I first enquired as to whether or not they were compulsory. The answer was 'of course' as though my question was a stupid one. But the evidence of my eyes belied what I was being told. Some people did have helmets but they wore them like bracelets over their wrists or strapped to the back of the saddle, never on their heads except in the case of rain.

In the last couple of years there has been a clampdown on all aspects of road safety and, if stopped by the police, a rider may be asked to put one on and if terribly unlucky be fined if the policeman is late for his siesta. But it is interesting that the main reason for not wearing crash helmets is not the heat or even a casual disregard for road safety, although these might be contributory factors. The real reason is that it is compulsory to wear one.

Freedom and Death (Captain Michalis in Greek) is an epic Nikos Kazantzakis masterpiece about the Cretans' revolt against their Turkish overlords in 1889. Its hero, Michalis, is the embodiment of a spirit that cherishes freedom more dearly than anything else. Greece has spent so much of its history subjugated to foreign powers that freedom is not taken lightly.

It is a matter of pride that people cannot be told what to do, even if that is to wear a crash helmet! There is no malice intended in breaking the law, hence the compromise illustrated by carrying the helmets instead of wearing them. Most Greeks are natural existentialists and their love of freedom at all costs can be illustrated by any number of the ways they routinely reject any kind of state-imposed authority.

Asklipio – A Picnic in Paradise

Just walking our picnic up to the car, which has to be parked outside the town of Lindos as there is no access for vehicles there, had taken its toll. The planned lie in and late start meant the sun was already giving off a 90 degree heat and our picnic lunch was far heavier than we had intended.

We had only met the local shopkeeper Poppy a few days previously, but on learning we were taking the short trip to Asklipio to see what we had been told were some of the most complete works of iconography on the island and to picnic near the castle ruins, she had arrived bearing gifts of water melon, cheese pies wrapped up in a tea towel, a Tupperware box stuffed with delicious honey cakes, a loaf of bread and a chunk of hard sheep's milk cheese. If that wasn't enough she also pressed us to take a half-gallon plastic container of honey-coloured wine!

All this, together with our more modest ham and salad baguettes, yoghurts and bottles of water were crammed into the boot of our tiny hire car before setting off southwards along the coast road. About ten miles into our journey in the rather upmarket, but sterile looking resort of Kiotari, we follow a sign telling us to turn right and head inland as we start our ascent to the small mountain village where we hoped to picnic.

Puffing and panting and relaxing by turns, our car makes its way through pine forests and olive groves growing on the remarkably lush hillsides before we arrive at the outskirts of this remote village. Shaped like an amphitheatre, the small traditional white houses cluster around a square dominated by the magnificent Church of the Dormition of the Virgin or Koimisis tis Theotokos, all giving audience to the castle ruins which look down on them from the mountain top.

Outside the church, beside its terracotta-tiled barrelled roofs and domes, stands a detached bell tower, like a four-tiered wedding cake topped with a cross. Built in 1060 this Byzantine church took the traditional cruciform shape before being later supplemented by two more modern apses to the south and north, which were added in the 18th Century to accommodate more worshippers.

The door was locked, but we were directed to a nearby house where an elderly retainer was more than pleased to open up for us. While the outside of this beautiful church exhibits a cool, clean honey-coloured façade, the inside reveals some of the most extraordinary, colourful frescoes I have ever been lucky enough to see. We had been told that the paintings here were the equal of those in the wonderful 14th-century Church of the Holy Virgin, which nestles in the alleyways of Lindos near the main square. The paintings there by the Symian master, Gregory, are stunning, but what was revealed on opening the door here was more than comparable. Light dapples the pebble-set chochlakia floor as it forces its way through the small windows illuminating and casting shadow in turn on the frescoes with which almost every surface seems ablaze.

Looking up inside the central dome, a massive chandelier stares back. The walls tell stories from the Testaments, beginning with creation through to the life of Christ, and the Dormition of Mary. The narrative expressed fills the interstices of the church with a vibrant reminder to the faithful that God is everywhere, even reminding the pious that the Last Judgement will some day come. I am no expert on ecclesiastical painting but, whatever one's religion, it would be difficult not to be moved by the passion expressed by the artists who created these murals.

Throughout the Orthodox world, a fast is held for the first fortnight in August in preparation for the feast for Theotokos, quite literally the bearer of God, or the Virgin Mary, to whom this church is dedicated, on the 15 August. I am struggling to find the names of the artists who worked here, indeed there is conflicting evidence as to the period from which they date, guesses range from the 15th to the 17th

Century AD. Whoever and whenever, a beautiful legacy has been bequeathed here.

Next door to the church are two tiny museums, one displaying more religious artefacts, the other a folk museum. Situated in the church's old olive press, this houses a wealth of agricultural equipment that has been used on the hills hereabouts over the centuries.

Returning to the car to retrieve our feast, we set off up the small road that leads to the castle ruins. Built by the Knights in the 15th Century AD, it is now little more than a ruin. At best a shell, two circular towers can still be discerned, but the serrated walls no longer hold fear for any would-be invaders. Inside the castle is overgrown with wild grasses and herbs, and evidence of it being an occasional impromptu corral for grazing beasts. Sitting on this spectacular outcrop, we picnicked looking down on the church we had just visited and out to the distant sea across hills where the rocks were punctuated with holm oak and wild herbs, the sun cajoling them to give off their fragrance. The occasional small chapel sat comfortably on the sparse, lazy landscape, which lay devoid of any sound as we ate and drank too much, unhurriedly enjoying the panorama spread out below.

A Healthy Debate

Much like back home, when people get together and are not discussing football or the economy, it is not long before talk turns to the state of the health service. It is amazing how, like the British, they can be fiercely critical on the one hand but also immensely protective of it on the other.

Numerous friends, family members and myself have had to use the Greek health service, and for the most part it is impressive. When I hear Greeks being critical it usually concerns, not the quality of care, but the distance needed to get to hospitals if you live outside a major urban area, and waiting lists for 'non-essential' treatment.

There is a severe shortage of nursing staff in many Greek hospitals and it is also true that if you are unfortunate enough to have to stay in hospital under the state health care system it is usually your family that are expected to provide non-clinical care.

For people who do not have anyone to look after them it is possible to employ a private nurse. Having said this, I have known people be taken ill in Greece while travelling alone and in the absence of family and friends have been looked after impeccably by hospital nursing staff.

There is a public health service in Greece and they must be doing something right because life expectancy in the country is one of the longest in the world, despite the people being some of the heaviest smokers on the planet; the country has also been recognized by the World Health Organization as having one of the highest quality health care systems although recently maintaining these high standards has become increasingly difficult under the government's austerity measures..

Nowadays, as in Britain, health care is free at the point of need and paid for by a national insurance scheme which covers workers and their families who have paid contributions and people from countries which have reciprocal healthcare arrangements, like those in possession of a European Health Card.

These services are generally administered by the IKA, a government body. Other social insurance and private funds also exist alongside the state system and these can gain the contributor access to doctors and clinics working in the private sector. Prescriptions written by doctors in the state system are charged at a maximum of 25 per cent of the cost and emergency dental care is free.

The Greek physician Hippocrates is considered the 'father of modern western medicine' and practiced back in about 400 BC, but in modern times it was action taken by the PASOK government of Andreas Papandreou in 1983 which made giant strides to establish the universal healthcare system. In not much more than a quarter of a century, the country has come a long way in their healthcare provision and, although the current financial crisis is putting the squeeze on services, they have much to recommend them at a time when a country like America is still debating the virtues of a system that is free for everybody when they are in need.

Myths and Legends of Rhodes

Rhodes appears more liberal in the distribution of its historical bounty than many of the other islands, which frequently set great store by the myths and legends prevalent in their ancient legacies. Although Rhodes shares its historical inheritance more equitably than other parts of Greece, its mythological endowment is not to be ignored. If legends pertaining to Rhodes are thin on the ground compared to other islands, those they have are big hitters and demand to be taken notice of.

The famous Colossus of Rhodes was the sculptural manifestation of Helios, the sun god born of the Titan Hyperion and his sister Theia. His story has been told many times and gained slight nuances of detail over time. One interpretation is this... Adorned with the sun as a shining halo, Helios arose each morning from a swamp in the east and drove his golden chariot pulled by nine, pure white, winged steeds who breathed fire as they galloped across the skies every day, before plummeting into the watery world of the Hesperides, over the western horizon. Here, adrift on the azure sea, was a ship aboard which his family waited for him.

Safely aboard, the ship would sail overnight, ready for the sun god to reappear in the east at dawn the next day.

His reliability in providing people with life-giving light meant he was absent when the Gods divided up the world into the domains over which they were each to preside. Angry at his omission, Helios sought out Zeus to complain, and was awarded an island which was just being born from the waves. He named it after a nymph with whom he was in love. Although in many areas of Greece Helios's identity became inseparable from the cult of Apollo, on the island which he named he was still held as a supreme divinity, celebrated by the ill-fated bronze statue fashioned by Chares, a task which drove the Lindian master sculptor to bankruptcy and eventual suicide.

No less tragic a fate was the destiny of Helen of Troy who also met her demise on Rhodes. Celebrated for her beauty, Helen's hand in marriage was sought by many suitors throughout the eastern Mediterranean. Each was made to swear to Helen's father, the canny Tyndareus, that they would come to the aid of the man who won her heart if ever he was in need. After three years of marriage to Menelaus the Mycenaean king of Sparta, a visit to her husband's court by Paris, the son of Priam the ruler of Troy, led to the favour being called in.

Abusing his hospitality, a besotted Paris abducted his host's wife and carried her off to Troy. Keeping their oaths, all the princes of Greece formed an alliance to put right this slight and, under the command of Menelaus' brother, Agamemnon, sailed to besiege Troy. Led by the mighty Hector, the Trojans held out for 10 years before they were undone by Greek cunning. Hidden inside a vast wooden horse a contingent of Greek warriors was pulled inside the walls of Troy by Trojan soldiers. Having breached their previously impregnable defences, the Greeks threw open the gates to the city from the inside and their armies poured in, killing and enslaving citizens and torching buildings. The 'face that launched a thousand ships' was reunited with her husband, but the conflict had created many victims and lived on in the memory of many who saw Helen as being responsible for the lives sacrificed to her cause.

On the death of her husband she was driven out of Sparta by two sons of Menelaus', legends differ as to whether or not they were her own offspring. Seeking refuge on Rhodes, she sought the protection of the queen, Polyxo. But her duplicitous friend bore a grudge against Helen as her husband Tlepolemus had lost his life fighting in the Trojan war. She commanded her servants to exact revenge, and one day, while Helen was bathing, she was seized and hanged from a tree. In Rhodes she is known as Helen Dendritis, which means Helen of the Tree. A sanctuary was built on the island in her name, but where this was I cannot find out, I suspect its location has been lost in the sands of time, but on the island the most beautiful woman who ever lived is still venerated.

The Oil at the Heart of Greece

Olives are the staple crop of Greece and are treated with great reverence. The plant is the most symbolic of Greece and has been harvested since the early Minoan period. At the ancient Olympic Games, winners were presented with an olive branch and it has since become a universal symbol of peace.

These tough plants can grow in a variety of locations and withstand the hot, arid summers but they are also hardy against winter cold. Everywhere in Greece will claim to produce the best olive oil in the country and, of course, Greek olive oil is always claimed to be the best in the world. There is some evidence to substantiate this claim. Italy imports Greek oil to blend with their own in order to get the acidity levels low enough for it to be marketed as extra virgin.

Greece produces about 12 per cent of the whole world's olive oil and, after Spain and Italy, is the third biggest producer. Having given up well over half of its cultivated land to growing olives, this land produces the largest number of varieties in the world.

But it is the quality of the oil that is so impressive. Most of it is extra virgin. For this reason, it is in such high demand that half of the crop goes for export. Much of that which is sold abroad is used to improve the quality of inferior foreign oils, although frequently, and often illegally, this is not mentioned on a bottle's labelling.

The olive harvest begins in the autumn. In the more northerly islands it starts in October, but further south it can be well into November, and lasts through until February of the following year. Nets are laid beneath the trees, and traditionally the branches are beaten with a stick to dislodge the olives that fall into the nets below.

Nowadays rotary poles powered by generators are frequently used to ease the backbreaking work. The olives are then loaded in sacks and taken to the press. Here they are crushed into a paste, usually by steel drums although more traditional operations use millstones.

This paste is then pressed to extract the liquid, a mixture of oil and water. In modern day production this liquid is placed in a centrifuge to separate the olive oil from the water. In some smaller-scale businesses the slower process of allowing gravity to separate the mixture is still employed.

For olive oil to be virgin it must go through this process and no chemicals be added either to help with manufacture or to adjust the flavour. The only difference between virgin and extra virgin oils is the acidity level that must be below 0.8 per cent if it is to make the grade as extra virgin, which more than 80 per cent of Greek oil is.

When you consider that in other countries that figure is nearer 10 per cent it validates the Greeks' claims to have the best quality olive oil in the world. This probably also accounts for the health-giving properties which are attached to the Greek diet, the Greeks living longer than any other people in Europe.

Greeks personally consume nearly twice as much olive oil in their diet as any other nation. On average each person uses 500ml every week. High in monounsaturated fats the oil is linked to a reduction in heart disease and helps lower cholesterol levels in the blood, in addition to its genuine life-enhancing properties it tastes marvellous. Good quality oil poured on a seasoned salad, or bread dipped in oil and vinegar must be one of the most blissful ways of getting healthier.

The oil is also used to make soap to sell mostly to tourists and for export, and olive wood is carved or whittled into salad bowls and chopping boards and many other tactile objects to be found in shops throughout the islands.

The Soul of Greece

If olives are the life-giving heart of Greece, then grapes are its soul. Vines abound throughout Greece. Although increasingly there are many large-scale commercial growing operations, often the vines are not the cut back, neat varieties seen in serried rows across the other winemaking nations of Europe. Free, untrained, the vines are frequently grown in small quantities to produce wine for personal consumption. This freedom for the vines to grow naturally probably accounts for the wide range of wine available and its variable quality.

The grapevine provides the four drinks synonymous with Greece, wine, raki (or tsikoudia), retsina and ouzo and the vine leaves do not go to waste either, they are stuffed to make a delicious *mezze*. Filled with rice, herbs, garlic and sometimes feta cheese then drizzled with some olive oil they are the perfect accompaniment to any of the aforementioned liquors.

One of the oldest wine-producing nations in history, there is evidence of vines growing in Greece going back more than 6000 years. Archaeologists found the remains of charred seeds and crushed grape skins during a dig on a Macedonian Neolithic site dated around 4500 BC. Ironically, during the time of the Roman Empire, wines from Greece were exported throughout Europe and North Africa. Today their presence abroad is limited, although strenuous efforts are being made to improve their marketability.

The best-known Greek wine abroad is Retsina. For many, this is an acquired taste, one I have so far failed to acquire. Best drunk cold, it is usually a white wine, but occasionally a rosé, which has pine resin added to it during the fermentation process. To me its smell is reminiscent of turpentine, although I cannot vouch that the taste is similar. However, Retsina is a popular drink throughout Greece and is readily available in supermarkets and off-licenses abroad.

A favourite by-product of the wine making process, is raki. All the discarded pieces of grape left over from the wine-pressing, the skins, stems and seeds, are fermented in barrels and then distilled to produce this clear spirit which can have an alcohol content approaching a very dangerous 90 per cent, but is more usually nearer 70 per cent.

Often raki is offered to guests as a sign of hospitality, served with fruit after a meal. It is also held to have medicinal powers and traditionally has been used as a cure-all for ailments both internal and external.

Most villages have a couple of people who have licenses to distil the liquor and this is usually an excuse for locals to get together for a celebration. This takes place about six weeks after the grape harvest in the autumn, allowing the fermentation process to weave its magic on the must residue left over from wine making. This is then distilled in copper vats over a bonfire, the whole production cycle frequently taking at least a weekend of sampling, eating and dancing.

Another favourite spirit widely drunk across Greece is made in a similar way to raki, but flavoured with aniseed. Ouzo is distilled from ethyl alcohol frequently made from grape must with added anise and other herbs and spices, which vary depending on the distillery. Its sweet liquorice taste is distinctive, and it can be drunk neat in shots or more usually with ice and water added, which gives the drink a milky colour. Like raki it is best to eat something while drinking as it is more-ish and deceptively strong.

The Greeks love to have a drink and their many celebrations throughout the year are always accompanied by copious amounts of alcohol but it is rare to see a Greek drunk. It is a point of honour to be able to hold your drink and it is unusual for food not to be eaten when out celebrating and for glasses of water to be drunk judiciously throughout.

Closer to God

In Rhodes you do not have to go very far without seeing a church. Often painted white, they can be glimpsed on top of mountains in some of the most inaccessible places. Still a deeply religious country, in Greece the church plays a major role in the lives of most families.

Greek Orthodoxy is noted in the national constitution as the prevailing religion of the country but the freedom to hold any religious belief is also enshrined in that constitution. It is, however, estimated that all but three per cent of the population consider themselves to be of the Greek Orthodox faith.

Families are the building blocks of Greek society, and at the heart of all of these families' life-changing moments and celebrations lies the church. Priests, or papas as they are known, are a common sight, going about their business in the community in their long robes and tall hats.

Although respected as being men of God, this gives them few special privileges in the eyes of the community and they are judged by the same standards as any of its other members. Priests are renowned for standing alongside their flocks.

Rather than being aloof they have a long history of fighting with them against the many forces of oppression Greece has faced.

An individual's relationship with the Almighty can be volatile. God can be berated and cajoled, shouted at and pleaded with but ultimately remains the focal point of life. Few Greeks would claim to be saints and, as in most societies, the richer they are the potential for them being less saintly is somewhat higher. As they get older, it is the need of some of these well-to-do sinners to repent, which accounts for the number of churches of various sizes built in the most remote spots.

In an attempt to pass through the eye of a needle, it is believed that by building a church, God will look more favourably on a sinner's repentance. Moreover, the further up a mountain the church is built, the nearer it is to God and the shorter the distance any prayers have to travel to be answered. These places of worship can vary in size from simple tiny chapels to larger, quite ornate, churches. Many of them are only used once a year on saint's days, but they are usually scrupulously maintained, often by local villagers.

Siege City – Ancient Ialyssos

Spread out beneath me as I stand on this hilltop is the whole of the north of Rhodes and its acolyte islands. At the edge of the summit lies the precariously placed remains of a fortress, finished off by allied bombing in the Second World War. Byzantine in origin, it is easy to see why the Knights further fortified this castle before succumbing to the forces of Suleiman the Magnificent, who in turn used it as a base to mount his siege of Rhodes Town. This ultimately put paid to the Knight's supremacy here.

From the nearby monastery that they had built on the site of an earlier 5th-century Christian basilica, the Knights made off with a priceless artefact, the Icon of the Virgin from the Church of Our Lady. That they set so much store in retaining the Icon when they scuttled from the island, gives some indication of its value. Unfortunately, we are never likely to see it as, when Malta was seized by the French in 1798, the then Grand Master of the Knights, Ferdinand von Hompesch, sent the priceless icon to the Czar of Russia for safekeeping. It was never returned, and following the Russian Revolution it was moved to Yugoslavia and has never been seen since.

Originally stolen by the crusading Knights from Jerusalem, the tragedy of the icon's subsequent loss is in no small part due to the belief that it was the work of the apostle St Luke.

But the history of ancient Ialyssos is rooted far further back in time. Considering this, it is surprising that the site is something of a hidden gem. Certainly this is the case when compared to the other towns of Lindos and Kamiros, which together with Ialyssos made up the ancient power base of Rhodes.

Indeed the site is so undersold that on my first visit to the island it passed me by entirely. I have to admit that I only decided to visit it at all on the spur of the moment, finding myself at a loose end after a rather than quicker than anticipated visit to the disappointing aquarium in Rhodes Town.

I suppose I shouldn't have been surprised that the Enydreio was oversold in the leaflet left under our car windscreen, and I am assured that it does do marvellous conservation work. Perhaps I have just been spoiled by the wow factor presented at other aquariums I have visited, but this left me underwhelmed. The building is impressive enough, an art deco edifice built in the 1930s by the Italians on the seafront at Ammos Point right on the northern tip of the island.

The aquarium itself is in the basement, and a person with an average attention span and without a severe mobility problem could be in and out within forty minutes. Suffice to say; emerging into the daylight, something was required to lift the mood.

We headed off on a voyage of discovery travelling south along the west coast. This side of the island was noticeably windier than the east coast, which probably accounts for the occasional disused windmill that still stands between the massive hotels that line the coast road. The hill of Monte Smith goes almost unnoticed as we pass behind its unassuming back, its face looking the other way surveying the grandeur of Rhodes Town. This somewhat unlikely named acropolis was previously known as the Hill of Agios Stefanos until, during the 1802 war against the incumbent Turks, a British Admiral, Sir Sydney Smith, set up a lookout post here, and left his name as a memento.

Fewer than two miles outside the city walls this 350-foot hill was the religious focus when the town was first created by the synoecism of the three city states in the 5th Century BC. Some columns of the 3rd-century BC Temple of Pythian Apollo stand as a reminder of its former glory, re-erected by the Italians. Lower down on the south side a more complete restoration has been done to a 2nd-century BC stadium and theatre, both of which I am pleased to say are still used for concerts and the staging of plays. A trip up to the summit is worthwhile just for the stunning panorama of the city and if you can make the climb just before nightfall, the sunset is inspirational.

Resisting the temptation to revisit the summit and take in the inexhaustible panorama of Rhodes Town we struck on, the crescent-shaped bay of Trianda unfurling in front of our eyes. The waves roll in here endlessly, breaking onto the broad sweep of the bay, making this village a hot-spot for windsurfers during the summer months. Among the modern tourist trappings can be found a reminder of Trianda's historic past. A row of houses by the roadside hides a mosque with its appended graveyard, giving a clue to a relatively recent event in the history of the village.

Known as Kritika, this small enclave was built in 1898 for Turkish refugees escaping from Crete when it became an independent state under the governance of Prince George of Greece. They were not the first settlers here by any means. The legacy of Trianda can be traced back to the Bronze Age, long before its prominence was usurped by the hill of Ialyssos where I am now standing. Like so many places in Greece, this is a land of legend, but in this case the story is more recent, being medieval in origin rather than of Ancient Greece. There is talk here of dragons, and the sources are impressive.

It was the German poet, philosopher and dramatist Friedrich von Schiller who popularised the myth. A great friend and contemporary of Goethe, his 1785 poem *Ode to Joy* became the basis for the rousing Fourth Movement of Beethoven's *Ninth Symphony*. From such an unimpeachable source comes the 1799 ballad *The Fight with the Dragon*, a poem which tells the story of the Knight Francisco Deodato de Gozon of the Hospitallers who slayed the Dragon of Malpasso on a nearby hillside.

If Schiller was to revel in this story, he was not the only scholar to relate it. More than a century earlier, another German, the famed Renaissance man Athanasius Kircher, recounted the myth in his weighty work *Mundus Subterraneus* between 1664 and 1668. In the chapter *De Draconibus*, Kircher references Bosius's *History of the Cult of St John of Jerusalem* telling the story of how a monster terrorised the local area, emerging from his quarry to consume young maidens.

So many knights had died trying to kill the dragon that the Grand Master proclaimed that on pain of death should any knight make any further chivalrous attempts to rid the island of its scourge. From Gascony, the warrior knight Francisco felt the shame of allowing this behemoth to wreak havoc with the island's young women keenly. He vowed to defy his master and confront the beast.

Meticulously the noble youth plotted his assault on the hereto-invincible leviathan, undaunted by its axe-like teeth, bulging eyes and blazing breath. He made a hideout in the surrounding hills, from where he spent days observing the monstrous beast as it part flew, part galloped after its hapless prey for whom any escape was impossible. The Knight then commanded his squire, foot soldiers and servants to construct him an exact facsimile of the dragon from paper and hemp which could be operated from the inside by his men in a macabre simulation of the evil demon.

He trained his horse and two huge brutes of hunting dogs to attack the monster without fear. When he had prepared himself and his animals he pulled on his best armour and, lance in hand and sword sheathed, he set out for the dragon's lair. His entourage were also armed with swords and medicine and secreted themselves in the surrounding rocks.

At the small local church, Francisco pledged himself to his order, and to God and set out for the dragon's cave. Sensing some easy prey the monster charged the Knight, but his horse stood its ground, and the dogs harried and tore at the monster's flesh and chewed off its genitals before the Knight impaled it on his lance.

With his scaly armour breached, the dragon, weakened through loss of blood, made one last frantic challenge to the now dismounted Knight. Rearing up on his hind legs he slashed at him with his giant claws until Francisco eyed his target and struck at the underside of the beast's neck. Split asunder and in his death throes the dragon launched his full weight at the noble youth, crushing him.

Running to their master, his servants revived him with water from a stream until he could mount his steed again and ride triumphant back to Rhodes Town. The reaction there was not all that he had anticipated and, instead of gratitude, the Grand Master had him thrown into jail for defying his cowardly edict and to stamp his authority over his disparate knights. But as word spread of the young man's bravery, public opinion turned, and the Grand Master was forced to bend to its will.

Released from his dingy cell, all his honours were restored, and such was his reputation that he was elected as the successor to the Grand Master, a position Francisco Deodato de Gozon of Gascony held between 1346 and 1353. The presence of the dragon reigned even longer as its skull is said to have been nailed above the d'Amboise Gate in the Old Town right up until 1837, in case anyone might doubt the efficacy of the story.

To get to the acropolis of ancient Ialyssos the road leaves Trianda sinuously invading the surrounding forest of pine which crowds the lower reaches of Mount Philerimos. Emerging into the light at the summit the site is somewhat incongruous, and for the purist perhaps there has been too much restoration.

So be it, but the Monastery of Our Lady of Philerimos, rebuilt by the Italians in the early part of the last century, stands as a fitting reproduction of the church originally built by the Knights, which itself stands on the threshold of the foundation of the 3rd-century BC Temple of Athena. The Knights built over a basilica, which had been consecrated by a 13th-century monk from the Holy Land who was named Philerimos, or 'friend to the wilderness' after whom the mountain was latterly named.

Prior to this the Mycenaean Greeks knew it as Achaia. More recently the Greek philosopher Strabo recalled it as Ochyroma (fortress), during the period Rhodes was part of the Roman Empire in the 1st Century BC. As well as a fortification, this valuable piece of high ground was also designated a place of worship.

Even the Temple of Athena is not the inaugural place of devotion to have graced this table-top limestone peak. Beneath it lies a Phoenician Temple, and who knows whether this was the first holy shrine to stand on the hilltop. Taking the tree-lined avenue near the entrance to the site and walking westwards past Italian relief images of stations of the cross, this Calvary leads to a huge concrete crucifix, which must be at least 50 feet in height, every inch of it a blot on this wonderful landscape. This however is but a shadow of the former cross, which stood approaching some 100 feet which was built by the Italians, but was destroyed during the Second World War by Allied bombs. Despite the brutality of the sculpting of this stark cruciform, the views that can be seen from the platforms accessed via a staircase inside leading out to the ends of the cross's arms are breathtaking.

To visit here now is to enjoy a peace that has so often belied this beautiful hill where knights, dragons and the Ottomans all staked their claim, and where the axis powers of Italy and Germany scuffled after falling out following the Italian surrender to the Allies in September 1943. There is much to see here for those interested in ancient archaeology and dreamers alike as the layers of history unfold, showing glimpses of themselves through the parched, scarred white limestone.

Greece's Street Food

It is something of an anomaly in a country that has the healthiest diet in Europe that the staple fast foods of Greece fall more into the category of comfort eating than healthy fare, and are none the worse for that. If you choose to indulge yourself with a moist, fatty gyros or a deep fried, honey-doused loukoumades you can do so in the knowledge that you can maybe salve your conscience with some grilled fish and salad at a later date.

A gyro is cheap and filling, and with just enough salad to make you believe, at least for second, that this heart attack in a wrap, might just have some redemptive qualities. The essentials that comprise a gyro is the way that the meat is cooked and what it is served in. Gyro means 'turn' and that is literally how the meat is cooked, on a vertical spit, in front of an adjustable heat source, the meat is then sliced off and served in a pitta bread. Most frequently pork, chicken is also sometimes used and they are usually topped off with tomato, onion, chips and tzatziki.

Wrapped in paper, the fat from this unctuous feast drips down the chin when eaten, just a few Euros buying a meal

Rhodes—A Notebook

which will keep most people satisfied for hours. Of Turkish origin, this Greek version of the ubiquitous doner kebab became popular during the Ottoman occupation of Greece. The meat on the spit is not one whole joint, but pieces and slices threaded onto the skewer and larded with strips of fat so it remains moist during cooking. Between the layers a spice mix of paprika, salt, pepper, garlic and herbs like oregano, and parsley are sprinkled. This is then trimmed to the familiar cylindrical shape and stored in a fridge ready for use. When cooking, the meat is cut off vertically from the rotating spit ready to load up the toasted pita parcels.

Loukoumades are the other, this time sweet, staple street food. Straight from the stove, these golden dough balls, deep-fried and flavoured with sugar or honey and cinnamon are delicious. The batter is just flour, yeast, salt and warm water left to prove for an hour before being deep fried, coated in a honey syrup, then sprinkled with cinnamon. According to the Greek poet Callimachus these sugary treats were served up as 'honey tokens' to the fortunate winners at the Olympic Games.

For as long as the novelty of these traditional dishes doesn't wear off, it is possible to eat well for very little in Greece, which is something I have often done, particularly when I was younger.

Bee Museum – A Taste of Honey

Rhodes boasts the only Bee Museum in the whole of Greece, although some might be surprised that there is one at all. But do not be put off, a visit here is more rewarding than I anticipated, and it does celebrate one of Rhodes' most famous products. Dotted all around the island are small, multi-colored wooden boxes, inside which liquid gold is created. The island's honey is considered by many to be the finest in the world, and it certainly does have a unique taste. Wild thyme and pine, among other indigenous plants on which the local bees graze, give the honey its distinctive aroma and taste. Rarely is it so good as eaten in the early morning sun with natural Greek yoghurt and nuts, or oozing out of baklava or almond and walnut kataifi pastries.

Beekeeping has been an occupation in Greece since prehistoric times and apiculture features in the works of Homer and Aristotle. Ancient myth has it that Aristeos, the son of the god Apollo, was taught the great Greek triumvirate of agricultural skills: cultivating grapes and olives, and beekeeping. He settled on the island of Kea in the Cyclades and passed on his skills to the natives there.

Nowadays, there are thought to be approaching 30,000 apiarists throughout Greece, of which only a fifth are engaged in full-time commercial operations. Nevertheless, Greece produces 17,000 metric tons of honey each year, the vast majority of which is consumed by the native population.

Hippocrates, the Greek father of western medicine, advocated the health-giving benefits of honey. It is still held to be good for the strength of bones, the health of body cells and neutralizing stomach acidity, as well as having antiseptic and antimicrobial qualities. But most importantly it tastes good.

As one of the most afforested places in Greece, much of the planting in Rhodes was done by the Italians in the first half of the 20th Century, particularly in the centre and south west of the island. It is here where non-native pines and eucalyptus took to the fertile soils and wear their veil of incongruity well. Driving the country roads near the castle of Monolithos, the freshest of honey can be found, tasted, and its provenance discussed with enthusiastic stallholders whose families have been harvesting this endemic treat for centuries. Buying direct from the forests where the bees collected the nectar used to produce the honey, somehow adds another dimension to its enjoyment. Whether a trick of the imagination or not, honey bought here, as well as tasting wonderful, can also transport you back to this tranquil corner of Rhodes, its taste redolent of the natural aromas of its source – pine, oregano, thyme…

The museum is owned by a large honey processing company and, as well as a well-stocked and tempting shop selling not just the raw product in its many forms, there are also sweets, cakes, soaps and candles all infused with local honey and beautifully presented. In the rooms next door are the exhibits, and I don't think we had to pay an entrance fee when we went.

The way the museum is curated tells the history of beekeeping, and artefacts from the last 200 years show the development of the trade. There are displays showing how apiculture has changed over the years and how modern techniques have been developed from age-old traditions such as handling beehives without getting stung and how the bees produce their valuable products of beeswax, royal jelly, propolis and, of course, honey.

It is inspiring to learn the different roles of each bee in their society, from the haughty, sole queen, fed a diet of pure royal jelly produced by the infertile female worker bees, and the several thousand drone males. The queen will fly to other colonies to get fertilized before returning to her own swarm to be nurtured and lay her eggs in the wax honeycomb cells made in the hive by the workers.

The queen can lay both fertilized and unfertilized eggs, with female workers and queens pupating from the fertilized and male drones from the unfertilized. The young workers, who feed them on a diet of royal jelly before they are weaned onto honey and pollen, sustain the larvae except in the case of a young queen. As they get older, the workers graduate to other tasks like guarding the hives, and receiving nectar and pollen from the forager workers, which they too will become in their dotage.

Honey is made from the nectar from the plants and trees harvested by the workers on their travels. Through a process of regurgitation from the bees' 'honey stomachs' they store the honey in cells as a food source. Beeswax is a secretion from the workers, who use it to build the wax combs where the larvae develop and honey is stored. Propolis, so valuable in the cosmetics industry, is a type of glue used by the bees to seal their hives and is made out of sap and resins from the forests. Bees can also be observed going about their business in transparent hives from which they fly out into the well-stocked gardens to forage for pollen and nectar. There is also a modern processing plant which, although closed to the general public, I believe can be viewed by appointment. Understanding how this age-old form of agriculture has developed and its links to the past from the modern world has added an extra dimension to my enjoyment of the end product that is so elemental to Rhodian culture.

Profitis Ilias – Little Italy

If the Italians sought to recreate the courtly era of the Knights through their reconstruction and renovation work on Rhodes, they also left one inconsistent legacy that smacks more of home-sickness than glories past. Profitis Ilias is a forested peak, the third highest on the island and named after the prophet Elijah. At just over 2,600 feet tall it is worth the drive to the top for the view alone. We approached it from the east coast road as we were staying in Lindos at the time, but it is actually closer to the western shoreline and taking the road for Salakos from Kalavarda, just a few kilometres south of the airport is another option.

Heading north along the coast through Archangelos, we took a left turn headed for Archipolis in the village of Kolimbia. If the architecture here appears a little different and the planning rather more regular than the organic growth seen elsewhere around the island, that is because Kolimbia was part of the Italian fascist obsession with order.

Originally named San Benedetto, Kolimbia was built as an experiment as a model village to house Italian settlers in the 1930s. It is reminiscent of the reclaimed Pontine Marshes south of Rome, where Mussolini built his agrarian utopia for

2000 loyal fascist families, usurping the indigenous poor who had previously lived there. It is of interest to stop and take it in, if only to be grateful that history prevented the extension of a madman's fantasies.

A more pleasing vista, but also the work of the Italians, lies inland of this 'model village'. Among a valley where plane trees and pines serve notice to the fertility of the soil is Epta Piges or Seven Springs. This tranquil retreat served both as a recreational getaway for the agricultural workers from Kolimbia and its environs, and also for the more practical purpose of being a supply of water for irrigation.

As its name suggests, hidden in this woodland sanctuary seven springs bubble up, feeding a small manmade lake via a narrow tunnel which it is possible to splash your way through in the dark. The walk takes the best part of ten minutes, wading through almost a foot of fast-running water in places and is not for the claustrophobic, but for those who take on the challenge it is supposed to banish all future fears. Emerging out the other end beside the beautiful lake feeding a waterfall with its cool blue-green water is a feast for the soul.

It is possible to avoid the tunnel by climbing above the entrance, crossing the road and following a footpath. In May it was not too busy, and we marked it down for the future as a perfect picnic spot if you don't mind sharing your lunch with the magnificent peacocks, which proudly strut their stuff around the tranquil waters of the lake. It is rumoured that the springs are everlasting and have never dried up, even in the hottest days of summer, but some dispel this myth claiming to have been there when the springs ran dry. When we went they were abundant enough for me to believe in their immortality, either way they certainly enrich the soul. Reluctantly leaving this magical enclave behind, we retraced our route back to the road that headed for Archipolis and the summit of Profitis Ilias.

Along this road is Elousa, a ghostly village which is haunted by memories of its seizure from the Greeks by the Italians who wanted the surrounding agricultural land to feed their growing emigrant population. Named *Campochiaro*, or 'bright fields' by the Italians, the name held a certain irony for the dispossessed Rhodians who, despite the not unpleasing nature of the Italianate architecture, have not been in any hurry to repossess their birthright.

If the influence of the Italian occupiers is overbearing around Elousa, just a mile and a half along the road, climbing upwards, is a tiny chapel so quintessentially Greek it stirs the emotions. At one with its surroundings this church, built in a cruciform shape, measures no more than 30 foot from apse to apse. Built in the 14th Century, and extended and embellished by successive generations, it is beautiful in its symmetry; the only deviation from this conformity a small bell tower over the west portal. A dome tops off this little gem of a chapel completing its visage with a simplicity that must have baffled those promoters of the fascist cause who plied their trade in these parts some 500 years later.

This is the Church of Agios Nikolaos Fountoukli, or St Nicholas of the Hazelnut. Not unlike that simple delicacy after which it is named, inside the shell lies a delicious delight. Frescoes dating from the 15th Century clamour for attention in all their faded glory. In the small space, I did not feel claustrophobic, but almost as though I was walking amongst the apostles and saints as they told their religious stories through these iconic representations.

Outside the church again, despite the blistering heat, it is easy to see what attracted the Italians to this part of the island. It is reminiscent of a south Tyrolean landscape, and it must have been with this in mind that they set about pruning and chopping the cedars and pines to create a parkland which was reminiscent of the Italian Alps. Had they not been so intent on manicuring the landscape, what is revealed as we approach the summit of Profitis Elias would be more surprising. Two large balconied chalets with dormered windows and pitched roofs emerge in a clearing among the trees. The Italians originally built these chalets as a hotel retreat for the settlers here, and any resemblance to the buildings of their Alpine homeland was entirely meant. They called this resort Villeggiatura, meaning holiday, the name being only a little less imaginative than the design of the buildings themselves. The only acknowledgement to the local environment was the names of the hotels, one being called *Elafos* meaning stag, the other *Elafina* meaning doe, the symbols of the island as represented by the bronze statues on the pillars either side of the entrance to Mandraki harbour in Rhodes Town.

When I last visited, the *Elafos* had been restored after years of neglect and hinted at something approaching its former glories with its 20 rooms and several suites, but the *Elafina* still stood in a state of neglect. Rumour has it that it too is to be restored, but in the current climate whether this will happen is a matter for conjecture. Don't get me wrong, this is a beautiful spot, and a visit can enhance the understanding of the mindset of the Italian settlers back in the first half of the 19th Century. I suppose my gripe is with the cultural imperialism, in Rhodes Town their architecture at least is restoration or pastiche, here it is totally out of character, but nevertheless charming in its way.

Close by the hotels is the church of Profitis Ilias itself, but it is not possible to reach the summit of the mountain as military shacks and communications aerials litter the fenced-off peak. But walking the rough tracks through the woods around the church and hotels, it is still possible to enjoy the cooler air at this higher altitude which promotes the growth of some spectacular displays of pink-tinged cyclamen and the white-petalled, clove-scented peonies with their golden hearts. These are the cousins of the Clusius peony which grow high on the slopes of the White Mountains in Crete, but here the host island is more benevolent, shaded, greener and cooler, more temperate in disposition. It is amongst this carpet of flowers, rather than beside the disconsonant chalets, that this spot reveals its true beauty. If the story told through the architecture left behind by the Italians fascinates, it is the primal, ingenerate landscape that captivates.

Epilogue

It is now April 2013 and it is almost three years since I wrote the article below. The precarious position of the Greek economy has since become even worse and the austerity measures forced on Greece by the Troika are still driving many people to the brink of despair and, sadly, beyond. That the protracted negotiations over the economy cost Georges Papandreou his job as prime minister is nothing to the price being paid by the ordinary Greek citizen who is finding the contraction of the nation's funds almost impossible to bear. And it is difficult to see where future growth will come from, although this month it has been reported that some indicators are showing a reversal of the downward economic trend. There is growing resentment against the governments of northern Europe, particularly Germany, who are seen to be dictating Greece's future and usurping her democracy.

If this bailout doesn't work, it is hard to countenance the alternative, default and a return to the drachma, which would float to find its own level. But with the rich already having squirreled much of their money out the country and the likely run on the banks that default would ensue things may only get harder, although many Greeks feel that at least it would mean they were in charge of their own destiny. But to my mind one of the most dangerous things about the new agreement is the installation by the 'Troika' of the EC, the European Central Bank and the International Monetary Fund, of officials in Athens to oversee the cuts. The worst thing that can be taken from a Greek is his pride, and these measures have deeply offended many Greeks.

The measures imposed are aimed to help the Greek government to cut its debt from 160% of GDP to a, still massive, 120% of GDP by 2020. There is still a risk that the measures taken will not be enough. I hope the optimistic reports that the financial measures are working are correct although elsewhere it is reported that the austerity medicine prescribed is in fact killing the patient. Here is what I wrote in 2011.

On 5 May 2010 three bank workers died in Athens during demonstrations against austerity measures proposed by the Greek government. The cuts were a condition of an EU financial bailout to rescue the country from bankruptcy and from defaulting on its already unserviceable debts.

The three staff, who were working at a branch of Marfin Bank, were killed when the bank was set on fire by demonstrators throwing Molotov cocktails. Most of the employees managed to escape, some were rescued from the roof of the building, but the three victims, including one pregnant woman, were not so lucky and were overcome by the fumes.

That other countries around the world were struggling in the wake of a global financial crisis brought about by the reckless lending and the unscrupulous selling on of debt packages by banks is no secret. Greece's problems went deeper. The crisis had exposed the true extent of the country's financial malaise.

For years the country had been borrowing far more money than it was earning in tax revenues. As early as 2001, when it joined the euro, it had managed to reach the required fiscal conditions by an economic slight of hand which saw its vast military spending somehow fall out of the financial ledger. Times were good and the auditors none-too-thorough.

All of a sudden the government had access to even more money at cheaper interest rates. Loan facilities they were to take full advantage of, particularly through the years leading up to their hosting of the Olympic Games in 2004.

With past Greek governments having been economical with the financial truth, fraud and bribery rife in the public services and an unwillingness of most Greeks outside the private salaried sector to pay any income tax, it was only a matter of time before the crisis came to a head. When in 2009 George Papandreou's PASOK party took over government from the right wing New Democracy party and opened the books they realized that the game was up.

But the international banking community had also wised up to Greece's dire financial condition, and fearing they might default on their outstanding loans or even go bankrupt, hiked up both their existing interest rates and those on any further borrowings.

Eventually the government reluctantly had to seek help from the EU, who alongside the IMF agreed to a 110bn euro bailout which has since escalated to 209bn euro. Even this did not prove to be enough, and not much more than a year later the financial institutions were still dubious that the country would be able to pay even the interest on the new loan. The EU and Greek government were now looking at a further advance and a rescheduling of the existing agreement.

The conditions attached to the bailout were going to be painful. Wage freezes, tax increases and both pension cuts and a rise in the retirement age were the requirements in an attempt to reduce the country's deficit from a staggering 14 per cent to less than 3 per cent of GDP.

This was always going to be a bitter pill for the people to swallow as they blamed the government for the fraud and mismanagement that had got them into the mess in the first place. This, coupled with the inherent dislike most Greeks have for authority, was always going to make any austerity measures challenging to implement to say the least.

Cutting government expenditure was only half the problem; the other side of the equation was collecting not just the new taxes but even the existing ones. It would not be unfair to say that the only sector contributing anything like their fair burden of the tax quota were salaried staff in the private sector who had it deducted at source. Public servants, privately owned companies and their employees all took advantage of the laxness in the auditing and collection services, indeed anyone paying anything like what they should be to the government was considered to be a mug.

A cash only, unreceipted economy had developed and the revenue services had neither the desire nor wherewithal to prosecute tax evaders. Where would they start? Indeed on the few occasions they pressed a claim, a bribe would usually see it quickly dropped. An example of how deeply rooted the trouble lies is doctors' salaries. Remarkably, despite them being some of the most highly paid people in the public and private sector, a large number of them fails to declare an income above the threshold that would mean they have to pay any tax.

Amidst a lot of finger pointing, people blaming government who, in turn, blame international financial speculators, only one thing is certain; there will be no easy solution. Getting back into the black will require a massive cultural shift that will be so unpopular and take so long that it is difficult to imagine a government sustaining a mandate to achieve it.

Many Greeks believe they should ditch the euro, default on their loans and return to the 'halcyon' days of the drachma. It is unlikely that this will happen as Greece's European partners have a vested interest in maintaining credibility in the euro. Any default on loans and return to the drachma would lead to rampant inflation and an economic free-for-all that would see many more casualties than winners.

And so it rumbles on; strikes, demonstrations, riots, everyone blaming someone else, and the deficit keeps on increasing. In other countries there is a legitimate debate as to whether they should spend their way out of recession or slash public spending. The first is not an option in Greece until the majority of people pay some meaningful taxes so the government has an income with which it can then cut its expenditure.

Meanwhile, ministers in the eurozone are delaying payment of the next 12bn euro tranche of the loan until they are more confident of the Greek government's privatization program and its ability to pull off the necessary cuts in public services.

The Greeks are proud people and it pains them to go cap in hand to Europe for loans. A lot of introspection will be required if this is going to be sorted. I hope it is, because the people deserve better.

As I write the TV news flashes up pictures of demonstrations in Athens. The EU is playing hardball with the Greek government. Georges Papandreou has appointed a new cabinet and has survived a vote of confidence to push through these tough measures. Can leaders of other members of the eurozone afford to let the Greek economy go under? The knock-on effect would likely create another world economic crisis. Many Greeks believe they should call the EU's bluff. Others believe that Greece should default on the debt and leave the euro.

The power workers are going on strike, petrol and food prices are rocketing and house prices falling. While pension contributions are rising, so is the retirement age and pensions themselves are dwindling. Many tourists are choosing to holiday elsewhere, frightened off by the media coverage and inflation.

Whatever happens, the Greek people have a long history of living through adversity. They will fight to retain their hard-won independence, democratic rights and standard of living, which they have struggled to achieve. Meeting the required austerity measures will be painful, but cutting themselves adrift from the euro would leave Greece without credit abroad and, for a country so reliant on imported goods, inflation would go through the roof.

I have just returned from the Ionian Islands and in a month will be heading further south to Crete. The people are stoically continuing life as they have always done. They are as welcoming as ever; their generosity of spirit towards the stranger remains unabashed. They face an uncertain future, but that is nothing new. When they look across the rugged landscapes of their benighted country, out over that peerless sea which binds them together, they know deep down that they are blessed to call it home – whatever their destiny.

With the rise of the extreme right in the form of Golden Dawn, the growing diaspora created by the economic climate and the real poverty being experienced by many citizens and the inability of social services to cope with the effects of the austerity measures, things look bleak. I hope the current solution works because a total collapse of the Greek economy is something that does not bear thinking about.

Get by in Greek

The following words and phrases are intended to give you a start at getting by in Greek. Use these, and your attempts at speaking the language will always be appreciated. The spellings used below are as close an approximation of words written in the Greek alphabet as I can get, as frequently no exact transliteration is possible. Dive in and have a go, a little Greek can go a long way…

Greetings and Courtesies
Hello *Yasas*
Goodbye *Adio*
Good morning *Kalimera*
Good evening *Kalispera*
Good night *Kalinichta*
Please/You're welcome *Parakalo*
Thank you *Efheristo*
OK *Endaxi*
Sorry *Signomi*
I don't understand *Then katalaveno*
Cheers *Issyia/Yamas*

Questions and Answers

Yes *Ne*
No *Ochi*
Where is? *Poo eene?*
How much is? *Poso kani?*
What is this? *Ti ine afto?*
Do you speak English? *Milate Anglika?*
What's your name? *Pos sas lene?*
What's the time? *Ti ora eene?*
How are you? *Ti kanete?*
Very well *Poli kala*
Not too bad *Etsi ketsi*
Not very well *Ochi ke toso kala*
I'm English/American *Eeme Anglos/Amerikana*
My name is Richard *Me lene Richard*

Weather

It's hot *Ti zesti*
It's cold *Ti krio*

Numbers

One *Ena*
Two *Dio*
Three *Tria*
Four *Tessera*
Five *Pende*
Six *Exi*
Seven *Efta*
Eight *Octo*
Nine *Enya*
Ten *Theka*

Fractions

Half *Miso*
Quarter *Tetrito*

Weights and Measures

Litre *Litro*
Kilo *Kilo*
Gram *Gramaria*

In the Taverna

I'd like *Tha ithela*
Could I have the bill please? *To logorizmo parakalo?*

Drinks

Beer *Bira*

Coffee *Kafe*

Juice *Himos*

Lemonade *Limonada*

Tea *Tsai*

Water *Nero*

Wine *Krasi*

Food

Beef *Vodino kreas*

Bread *Psomi*

Butter *Vootiro*

Cheese *Tiri*

Chicken *Kotopolo*

Eggs *Avga*

Fish *Psari*

Fruit *Froota*

Ham *Zambon*

Lamb *Paidaki*

Meat *Kreas*

Milk *Ghala*

Pork *Hirinio kreas*

Potato *Patata*

Salad *Salada*
Steak *Brizola*
Sugar *Zachari*
Vegetables *Laxanika*

Useful Words

Airport *Airodromio*
Bank *Trapeza*
Bad *Kakos*
Big *Megalo*
Bus stop *Stasi*
Car *Aftokinito*
Church *Eklisia*
Come here/in *Ella*
Doctor *Iatros*
Garage *Garaz*
Hospital *Nosokomio*
Let's go *Parme*
Little *Ligo*
Mobile phone *Kinito*
Petrol *Venzini*
Petrol station *Statio venzinathiko*
Pharmakio *Pharmacy*
Photograph *Photographia*
Postbox *Gramatokivotio*

Postcard *Kart postal*
Room *Thomatio*
School *Skolio*
Shower *Doosh*
Stamps *Gramatosima*
Sun *Ilios*
Ticket *Isitirio*
Today *Simera*
Toilet *Toiletta*
Tomorrow *Avrio*
Tonight *Apopsi*
Rain *Vroxi*
Wait *Perimene*
Well *Kala*

The History of Rhodes At-a-Glance

Here is a brief synopsis of the major events in Rhodes' history. For some of the ancient history the dates are approximate, as exact dates in many cases have not been established.

- **7000 BC** Neolithic Period.
- **2800 BC** Early Helladic Bronze Age civilization, Greek mainland.
- **1800 BC** Proto-Greek speaking tribes, forunners of the Mycenaeans, arrive on Greek mainland.
- **1600 BC** Minoans settle on Rhodes.
- **1500 BC** Mycenaeans invade Rhodes.
- **1200 BC** The Trojan Wars.
- **1100 BC** Fall of the Mycenaeans displaced by Dorian Greeks.
- **1000 BC** Classical Greek period begins.

800 BC	Dorians establish ancient settlements of Lindos, Ialyssos and Kamiros.
750 BC	Homer writes *The Iliad* followed 20 years later by *The Odyssey*.
505 BC	Democracy introduced in Athens, making way for the Classical Greek period.
478 BC	Rhodes invaded by Persian forces but liberated again by an army from Athens. Rhodes joined the Athenian League.
408 BC	The cities of Lindos, Ialyssos and Kamiros unite to build the new capital city of Rhodes Town.
384 BC	Birth of Aristotle.
356 BC	Birth of Alexander the Great.
340 BC	Persians conquer Rhodes.
332 BC	Alexander the Great defeats the Persians and Rhodes is assimilated into his empire.
323 BC	Alexander the Great dies, Hellenistic period begins. Rhodes forms an alliance with Egypt.
305 BC	Macedonian King Demetrius lays siege to Rhodes. Defeated, his abandoned siege engine is sold for scrap and the proceeds used to build the Colossus.
280 BC	Completion of the Colossus.
226 BC	Massive earthquake destroys the Colossus.

200 BC	Second Macedonian War ending in 196 BC with Rhodes remaining independent.
164 BC	Rhodes formally becomes part of the Roman Empire.
33 AD	Crucifixion of Christ.
50 AD	St Paul brings Christianity to Rhodes on his Third Mission.
286 AD	The Roman Empire divides into East and West creating the Byzantine Empire.
600 AD	Rhodian Sea Law instigated throughout the Mediterranean.
654 AD	Rhodes occupied by the Islamic forces of the Umayyad dynasty, the remains of the Colossus is sold for scrap.
674 AD	Rhodes sacked by Arab forces but later abandoned after their fleet was destroyed by Greek attack and sunk in bad weather. Rhodes returns to the Byzantine Empire.
1090 AD	Rhodes captured by Turkish forces.
1099 AD	First Crusade, Rhodes recaptured by the forces of Byzantine emperor Alexios Komnenos.
1204 AD	Fourth Crusade left Byzantine Empire in disarray.
1248 AD	The Genoese occupy the island.

1250 AD   The Genoese ousted by Nicaean forces. Rhodes becomes part of Nicaean Empire.

1309 AD   The Knights Hospitaller occupy the island, becoming the Knights of Rhodes and ending the Byzantine era.

1444 AD   Rhodes besieged by the Sultan of Egypt but his forces are repulsed by the Knights.

1480 AD   Ottoman forces under Sultan Mehemed II defeated.

1522 AD   Suleiman the Magnificent defeats the Knights.

1523 AD   The Knights negotiate safe passage to Crete before moving on to Malta. Rhodes becomes part of the Ottoman Empire.

1821 AD   Greek revolution and declaration of independence, although this was not fully achieved for eight years.

1832 AD   Prince Otto installed as King of Greece (at this time The Peloponnese, Athens, The Mani and the islands of the Saronic Gulf, Cyclades and Sporades).

1912 AD   Italy seizes Rhodes from Ottoman Turks.

1923 AD   Greco-Turkish population exchange, West Thrace becomes part of independent Greece.

1939 AD   Start of Second World War.

1940 AD Following 'Ochi Day' Greece is invaded by the Axis powers.
1943 AD Italy signs Armistice, Germany invades Rhodes.
1944 AD Gestapo send most of Rhodes's Jewish population to the death camps.
1944 AD Start of Greek Civil War.
1947 AD Rhodes becomes part of independent Greece.
1949 AD Greek Civil War ends.
1952 AD Greece joins NATO.
1967 AD Coup of the Colonels.
1974 AD Cyprus crisis, collapse of the military dictatorship.
1975 AD New republican constitution becomes law.
1981 AD Greece joins European Community.
2009 AD Debt crisis plunges Greece into civil unrest.

Greek Food At-a-Glance

The following list is by no means exhaustive, but I hope it gives a flavour of the foods on offer in Crete.

Appetizers, Starters and Mezzes

Dolmades Stuffed vine leaves

Sardeles pastes Salted sardines

Gavros marinates Anchovies in oil, lemon and herbs

Saginaki Deep fried cheese

Saginaki garides Shrimp with cheese and tomato sauce

Revithia keftedes Deep fried chickpea balls

Tsatsiki Yoghurt, cucumber and garlic sauce

Taramasalata Blended fish roe, oil and lemon salad

Kolokythokeftedes Fried courgette balls

Tyrokeftedes Fried cheese balls

Boksades Lamb cubes with feta cheese in pastry

Spanakopita Spinach pie

Tyropita Feta cheese pie

Skordalia Garlic, potato and lemon sauce

Fava Split pea, garlic and lemon sauce

Salads

Horiatiki salata (Greek country salad) Tomatoes, onion, cucumber, feta cheese and olives

Ampelofasoula salata String bean, tomato and olive salad

Patatasalata Potato, onion, parsley and olive salad

Lahanosalata Cabbage, carrot, garlic and lemon juice salad

Garidosalata Shrimp salad

Meat Dishes

Mousaka Aubergines, mince, potatoes and béchamel sauce

Kotopolo me patatas sto forno Roast chicken and potatoes

Arni me patatas sto forno Roast lamb and potatoes

Souvlaki Grilled meat, usually lamb or chicken on skewers with peppers, onions and tomatoes

Gyros pitta Sliced grilled pork, chicken or lamb in pita bread with salad chips and tsatsiki

Sofrito Veal with wine, garlic and parsley sauce

Kleftiko Slow-cooked lamb with potatoes, garlic, oil and lemon juice

Paidakia Grilled lamb chops

Keftedes Deep fried meatballs

Macaroni me kima Pasta with minced beef, garlic and onion

Beefteaki Seasoned minced beef patty

Sousoukakia Seasoned, grilled minced-beef balls in tomato sauce

Brizole Steak

Pastisada Veal, tomato and onion stew with spaghetti

Tomates gemistes Tomatoes stuffed with minced beef and onions

Moschari stifado Veal stew with tomatoes and onions

Kotopolo me portokali Slow-cooked chicken in orange juice

Gemista Baked peppers and tomatoes stuffed with rice and herbs

Saligaria me ryzi Fried snails with rice

Fish Dishes

Garides Shrimps

Mydia Mussels

Barbounia Red mullet

Ksifias Swordfish

Gavros Anchovy

Kalimari Squid

Astakos Lobster

Kolioi Mackerel

Bakaliaros Cod

Maridaki Whitebait

Sardeles Sardines

Lakerda Tuna

Psarasoupa Fish soup
Psari plaki Baked fish

Puddings and Pastries

Loukoumades Deep-fried dough balls with honey and cinnamon

Pastelli Honey and walnut wafers

Amydalopi Almond cake

Baklava Filo pastry with cinnamon, walnuts and honey

Kataifi Almond and walnut pastry with syrup

Yaourti me meli Yoghurt and honey

Risogalo Rice pudding

Extract from Crete – A Notebook

Vai – A Tropical Paradise?

I knew nothing about Crete before first arriving back in the early 1980s. If I had one image in my mind before I came here it was of palm trees on a deserted beach of golden sand. I don't know what planted this picture in my imagination but it pretty much fits the bill of the palm forest of Vai in the far east of the island. Perhaps I had unconsciously seen a picture of this startlingly mesmeric corner of Crete in a magazine article; or maybe I had confused Crete with some Caribbean idyll – but the pictures in the windows of the travel bureaux along 25 August Street in Heraklion repeated this stunning image.

Unfortunately, at that time, the picture was more of the dream than the reality. In the Seventies, hippies who had been driven out of their previous communes in the caves of Matala on the south coast of the island had appropriated the beach and adjoining forest. Numerous itinerant backpackers joined them, and the lack of facilities led to what had become a giant campsite turning into a rubbish dump.

Carrier bags, cigarette packets, bottles and cans were among the detritus that littered this small piece of paradise on top of which was pitched a small shanty town of tents and ramshackle shelters. On my first trip here, after a long, hot, three-hour bus ride to Sitia from Heraklion and a further trip taking the best part of an hour, the state of the beach left me totally disillusioned, my dreams shattered.

The land is owned by the Monastery of Toplou, an imposing building lying some five miles inland of the forest, and the monks and government authorities recognized that something needed to be done. They restored the beach and forest to its natural state and, under an EU directive, it became a protected site administered by the Greek Forestry Commission. All camping along with any activity which is thought could endanger this fragile environment is banned.

Visiting nowadays it is apparent that the measures taken have been successful. So much so that in the summer the litter lying on the beach has been replaced by thousands of tourists, bussed in from resorts across the island to see what is the largest palm forest in Europe. The 300,000 square yards of Cretan date palms is endemic to the island and have been growing in the area for as long as there is recorded history.

The name Vai is derived from the word vayia, which means palms in Greek.

To the edge of the beach lie some steps which lead up to a viewing platform. Reaching this point you can see a panorama of the whole beach and forest spread out in front of you. The depth of the blue of the sea is unfathomable as it nudges up to the honey gold sands fringed by the verdant fronds of the palms. A tiny island floats in the middle of the bay wrapped in the encircling embrace of the hot sands and shady palms on the shoreline

The reputation of this spot of outstanding natural beauty is such that it is, like with many other places on the island, best to come out of season. If that is impossible, then visit early or late in the day to avoid the crowds. I made the mistake once of taking some friends who were visiting in late July, after I had sung the praises of Vai's beauty. From arrival at the rammed car park, which was as packed as the beach itself where sunbathing bodies obscured every square inch of sand, it must have been hard for them to relate this to my description of a balmy idyll.

Some quick thinking and a suggestion that we visited Moni Toplou rescued me. Moni means monastery, in this case that of the aforementioned order who own the land. We retraced our route driving out of the full car park, navigating past cars now parked in any higgledy-piggledy fashion in anything vaguely resembling a space on the access road. Cars hooted at pedestrians and double-parked coaches stopped to disgorge their cargo of sun-seeking passengers.

Leaving behind the mayhem of the beach we drove the five miles or so back inland to the magnificent monastery. At first sight, the face the monastery shows to the world is not one of a peaceful retreat. It is built for war, and resembles a fortress, dominating the surrounding hot, arid landscape. On closer scrutiny of the history of Moni Toplou or Panagia Akrotiriani (Our Lady on the Cape) as it is otherwise known, it becomes apparent that the building needed to be strong to defend it against any number of antagonists over the centuries. Its very name, Toplou, is derived from the word 'top' in Turkish, which means cannon, referring to weapons which had been employed during Venetian times to defend the order against the marauding Turks. And the order's history is littered with examples of them being subjected to siege, plundering and persecution.

The outside walls suggest this violent history. There has been a monastery on the site since the 14th Century but this was thought to have been razed to the ground by pirates. Following its demise it was rebuilt in the 16th Century only to suffer looting at the hands of the Knights of Malta in 1530 before being destroyed again, this time by the catastrophic earthquake of 1612. Undeterred the ruling Venetians collaborated with the monks to build the current structure to sure up the defenses of this remote part of Eastern Crete. Following the demise of the Venetians and their surrender to the Turks in 1646, the monastery fell into disrepair before being resurrected under special privileges obtained from the then ruling Ottomans. This special relationship was not to last. During the independence uprising in 1821 the participation of the resident monks led to their wholesale slaughter by the Turks. With the monastery inhabited again by 1828, the order was once more routed by the Turks in the 1866 revolution. The bloodshed did not end there; during the Second World War the monks continued their proud tradition of independence and gave shelter to both Cretan and British freedom fighters. When a radio transmitter hidden in a cave near the monastery was discovered, the Germans arrested two monks and the abbot. One monk succumbed to torture and died in prison while the other monk and the abbot were both executed.

Outside the fortified walls I turned and looked around this desolate and windswept plain. On a hill in the background turned giant wind turbines, the modern incarnation of the lone mill, its sails long since gone, which remained the sole building outside the main monastery walls, apart from the small chapel which marked the monks' graveyard. I turned back to the imposing gates above which openings in the walls through which boiling oil was poured on attackers can be seen. On entering, the monastery showed a different, more benign face. The interior courtyard that stands in the shadows of the 33-foot-tall fortified walls is paved with pebbles, smoothed by the sea before being layed here and being further burnished by centuries of the monks to-ings and fro-ings. The cloisters surrounding the central courtyard are bedecked with pottery urns from which flourish an abundance of flowers of every conceivable hue. A stairway leads up to the cells where the three blue-robed monks and the abbot now in residence retire when they are not working, dining in the refectory or at prayer in the church which is topped with the imposing square bell tower with a domed belfry standing 110 feet tall. Inside is an icon by the 18th-century master Ioannis Kornaros, his 1770 work 'Great Art Thou, O Lord, and Wonderful Are Thy Works', comprises four central pictures surrounded by 57 individual miniature biblical scenes illustrating a line from the Orthodox prayer of the icon's title.

Leaving the dark interior of the church, our eyes blinking as they readjust to the blinding light, we notice an inscription in the wall of the church. This, I later discover, is the verdict handed out by a court of arbitration in Asia Minor called Magnesia, which had been called upon to rule on a dispute over land rights during the Roman occupation of the island in the 2nd Century BC. The factions involved were Cretan tribes from nearby Itanos and from further to the south west

Ierapytna, now Ierapetra. For what it's worth, the ruling went in favor of the local Itanos clan but the inscription itself had been discovered by the British classicist, mathematician and writer Robert Pashley in 1834 who found it being used as a headstone in a graveyard and suggested it be given pride of place set in the wall.

The monastery also has a small museum containing engravings made by monks from Mount Athos on mainland Greece and exhibits a number of 15th-century icons of the Constantinople School. Although only four members of the order remain living here, the wealth of land, over which the monastery presides, produces wine, raki and olive oil, all of which are available for sale in a small shop on site.

Crete – A Notebook is available in paperback and kindle format from Amazon.com & Amazon.co.uk and is available in all other eBook formats.

Extract from The Greek Islands – A Notebook

To Kefalonia by Boat

The July sun was just starting to signal its intent for the day ahead as we made an early morning start from the harbor at Vasiliki. When past the harbor wall, Georgos pushed the throttle forward and the rib inflatable rose up onto a plane, thrust out of the water by the enormous twin outboard motors mounted on the stern. The boat flattened out and skimmed effortlessly across the flat calm Ionian as Lefkada rapidly became an outline of cliffs on the horizon.

We were heading for Kefalonia, the largest of the Ionian archipelago, which lies just 10 nautical miles south of Lefkada. The breeze created as the rib flew forward was welcome and the odd bit of spray thrown up when the boat encountered wash from passing shipping helped neutralise the effect of an already scorching sun.

It takes the ferry from Vasiliki an hour and a half to travel the distance between the two islands but in these calm conditions, at full throttle in the rib, we made the passage in somewhat under half an hour. We entered a deserted bay only accessible by boat where the cliffs rise vertically off the beach. No paths run here so we had it all to ourselves. The beach is in the shade of the backdrop of rocks but the water is still like a warm bath.

We anchored up and rolled backwards off the inflatable tubes to snorkel in the crystal clear water. I don't know whether it's the bay's relative isolation, or the shade provided by the vertiginous shoreline but the waters provide a haven for the most dazzling array of fish, a rainbow of colors shoaling across the rocks and golden sands beneath us.

I returned to the rib for some fish pellets, and dived down among the larger fish holding out my hand. Remarkably unafraid they darted in to feed, grabbing the food before retreating back to rejoin their shoal.

Climbing back into the boat we lay in the sun to dry off before setting out to sea and around the headland at the northernmost tip of the island into the channel that separates it from its neighbor Ithaca. Going more slowly now, we could take in the stunning shoreline as we headed south.

The hilly landscape is a patchwork of olive groves and cypresses. A small car ferry crossed ahead, its wake causing the bow to momentarily slap up and down, sending more refreshing spray flying into our faces.

We turned inland following the course of the ship. Up on a hill is a tall, rectangular, grey stone lighthouse and below it, down the hillside, a much shorter, squat cylindrical structure. This, Georgos explained, is the old 16th-century Venetian lighthouse that was decommissioned when the taller, more visible tower replaced it in 1892. This is the light that still guides boats into the small harbor of Fiskardo that we were now entering.

To our right the ferry had moored bow first to its small quay and its crew were winching the ramp down for its cargo of cars and foot passengers from Lefkada to disembark. The rest of the small harbor is picture perfect. Multi-colored fishing boats bob up and down on their moorings, nets glistening on the decks and red and yellow buoys tied to their rails. Among them, moored stern in, are flotillas of sailing boats and privately owned yachts and motorboats of all shapes and sizes.

Skirting the L-shaped harbor are a cluster of traditional 18th-century Venetian-built houses, tavernas, cafes and shops painted in a multitude of pastel shades, providing the backdrop to this busy village; fishermen, waiters and tourists all going about their business in the mid-morning sunshine. Rising up behind the waterfront houses, the surrounding hills are densely populated with rich forest, only broken by the occasional villa set in a clearing overlooking the straits.

We rafted up alongside a couple of other boats and took a stroll through the winding streets. We walked under the shade of numerous striped awnings and sprays of bougainvillea of every hue, which overflowed from the balconies above. Fiskardo is one of the more fortunate among towns and villages on the island in that its buildings survived the terrible earthquakes of 1953 which caused so much devastation elsewhere.

In August of that year, four earthquakes hit Kefalonia. The largest, measuring 7.3 on the Richter scale had its epicenter directly below the southern end of the island and destroyed the majority of buildings in the area. This, following the devastation wreaked on the island a decade earlier in the Second World War, means that many of the buildings are relatively modern.

The terrible history of Kefalonia during the war is well known, not in the least as a result of the English writer Louis de Bernieres' 1994 novel Captain Corelli's Mandolin. The book and the subsequent film released seven years later tells the tale of the developing love between Pelagia, the daughter of the local doctor, and Antonio Corelli, a captain with the occupying Italian forces.

This fictional story is set against the remarkable events that unfolded after the invasion of Greece by the Axis powers. Enemy forces that mostly comprised Italian personnel, along with a much smaller German contingent, occupied Kefalonia. Following Italy's armistice with the Allies in September 1943, the Italian forces sought to return home.

The German command however, not wanting Italian weapons to fall into the hands of the islanders, demanded they be surrendered to them. Not trusting the Germans to let them go, the Italians refused to hand over their arms and dug in awaiting evacuation while the Germans sent reinforcements to the island.

The former allies were now at war with one another and the fighting came to a head with the siege of the capital, Argostoli. After brutal hand-to-hand fighting in the streets, the town fell to the German forces. Of the surviving Italian troops, around 5000 were subsequently massacred as a reprisal by the Germans.

De Bernieres' book has in no small way added to the island's popularity as a tourist destination. The subsequent building of more facilities to accommodate and service that trade, has been welcomed as a valuable source of income by most of the islanders. Fiscardo itself, however, has been spared much of such redevelopment. Planning regulations and conservation laws protect both its architectural heritage and the outstanding natural beauty of the surrounding hills.

We sat down at one of several quayside tavernas, to a plate loaded with seafood. Mullet, herring, mixed small fish and prawns grilled with herbs and sprinkled with olive oil and lemon juice were accompanied by bread dipped in oil and vinegar, olives and a beer.

In contrast to the earlier passage, the return journey to Lefkada proved to be livelier. The afternoon wind rose noticeably as we left the shelter of the channel between Ithaca and Kefalonia and powered northwards into the open sea. The waves had turned into rollers and at high speed the rib would take off between crests, slamming down on landing before surging forward again to meet the next peak.

Going flat out we got drenched and the salt spray stung as it hit and made the eyes sore. Wearing sunglasses for protection was not an option as they would be blown off in the wind or washed off by the bow waves. At lower speeds the boat would wallow and slam, jarring the back continuously. We opted for the high-speed option and just enjoyed the adrenaline rush. Georgos was a master of the conditions and his confidence made the whole experience exciting rather than terrifying.

The wash from passing ships had to be treated with more respect in these conditions and met bow on, so as not to risk capsizing. The wind-speed gauge was reading about 30 knots as we suddenly came into the lee of Lefkada and the sea conditions moderated as we approached the small harbor of Vasiliki. Hundreds of windsurfers were out just off the shallow sloping beach showing off their spectacular skills in the testing conditions. Soaked and exhilarated we climbed ashore, on the lookout for a cold drink to get rid of the taste of salt water.

About the Author

Richard Clark is a writer, editor and journalist who has worked on an array of national newspapers and magazines in the UK. In 1982, on a whim, he decided to up sticks and go and live on the Greek island of Crete. So began a love affair that has continued to this day, when he still visits the Greek islands on a regular basis. He is married with two grown up children and lives in Kent.

Printed in Great Britain
by Amazon.co.uk, Ltd.,
Marston Gate.